True Stories From the History of Ireland: [1st-] 3d Series

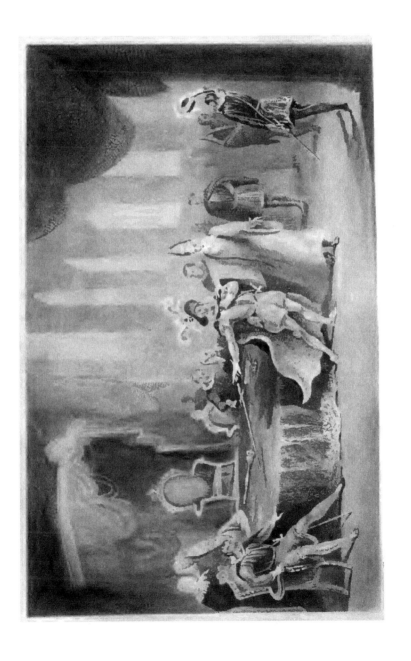

HISTORY OF IRELAND.

BY

JOHN JAMES McGREGOR

SECOND SERIES

CONTAINING THE MEMORABILIA OF IRELAND UNDER THE TUDORS

MAYNOOTH CASTLE 1829.

DUBLIN
WILLIAM CURRY JUN. & Co.
1829

TRUE STORIES

FROM THE

HISTORY OF IRELAND.

BY

JOHN JAMES M'GREGOR,

AUTHOR OF "A HISTORY OF THE FRENCH REVOLUTION,"
&c. &c.

SECOND SERIES,

CONTAINING

THE MEMORABILIA OF IRELAND UNDER THE TUDORS.

SECOND EDITION.

DUBLIN:
WILLIAM CURRY, JUN. AND CO.
9, UPPER SACKVILLE-STREET.

1833.

DA
911.2
M17 t
v.2

CONTENTS.

CHAPTER I.

IRELAND UNDER THE TUDORS.

PAGE

Accession of Henry VII.—Aversion of the Irish to his Government—Imposture of Lambert Simnel—He arrives in Dublin—The Lord Deputy Kildare proclaims him King, by the name of Edward VI.—General Defection of the Irish—Loyalty of Waterford—Intrigues of the Duchess of Burgundy—Arrival of Flemish Troops in Dublin—Coronation of Simnel—The Impostor invades England—Battle of Stoke—Capture and Degradation of the mock King—Arrival of Sir Richard Edgecombe—Submission and Pardon of the Earl of Kildare—Feuds in Ulster.   1

CHAPTER II.

Pretensions of Perkin Warbeck to the Crown of England—Kildare removed from Office—Walter Archbishop of Dublin, Lord Deputy—Perkin Warbeck at Cork—Maurice (Ballingarry) Earl

CONTENTS.

of Desmond—Perkin retires to France—The Sweating Sickness—The Archbishop of Dublin's interview with King Henry—Memorial on the miserable state of Ireland—Sir Edward Poynings, Lord Deputy—O'Hanlon's Insurrection—Kildare suspected—Poyning's Parliament—Attainder of Kildare—Return of Perkin Warbeck—Siege of Waterford—Repulse of Warbeck and the Earl of Desmond—Subsequent Adventures and Death of Perkin Warbeck—Kildare committed to the Tower—Kildare and the Bishop of Meath before the King—Kildare's singular triumph — Murder of Lord Barry.. 25

CHAPTER III.

Commotions in Ulster—Kildare restored to the office of Lord Deputy—His vigour and success—Interview between Kildare and Sir James Ormond at St. Patrick's Cathedral—Battle of Knocktuadh—Nugent, Lord Delvin—Defeat of the Bourkes— Capture of Galway—Extraordinary Instance of Civic Justice exemplified in the Story of Lynch, Mayor of Galway—Death and Character of Henry VII......................... 46

CHAPTER IV.

Accession of Henry VIII.—Death of the Earl of Kildare—Vigorous conduct of Gerald, his son and successor in the Government—New Feuds between the Geraldines and Butlers—

CONTENTS.

PAGE

Margaret, the great Countess of Ormond—Kildare accused — His interview with Cardinal Wolsey—Anecdote of Kildare—The Earl of Surrey Lord Deputy — Insurrection of Con O'Neil—Submission of O'Neil and O'Donnel—O'More's Insurrection—Surrey's Popularity and Recal—The Irish in France—Exploits of Nicholas Walsh—Pierce (Rufus) Earl of Ormond, Lord Deputy—Murder of Talbot of Belgard—Dissentions between Ormond and Kildare—Kildare Lord Deputy— Treasonable practices of Desmond—Kildare suspected and summoned to London — Pierce Earl of Ossory restored to power—Murder of the Bishop of Leighlin—Machinations of the Emperor Charles V.—Sir William Skeffington Lord Deputy—Kildare restored — His ambitious and violent conduct—Secret proceedings of the Council — Kildare summoned to London — The Government is committed to Lord Thomas Fitzgerald—Rumours of Kildare's Execution—Insurrection of Lord Thomas Fitzgerald—Action at Salcock Wood—Murder of Archbishop Allan—Correspondence between Fitzgerald and Lord James Butler—Siege of the Castle of Dublin—Repulse of Fitzgerald—Arrival of Sir William Skeffington—Siege of Maynooth—Final suppression of the Insurrection—Death of the Earl of Kildare—Lord Leonard Grey Lord Deputy—Execution of Lord Thomas Fitzgerald and his five Uncles—Escape and Adventures of young Gerald Fitzgerald.... 63

CONTENTS.

PAGE

CHAPTER V.

Alterations in Religion—Obstacles to the Establishment of the King's Supremacy in Ireland—Archbishop Browne — Opposition of Primate Cromer to the new changes—The Parliament declares the King Supreme Head of the Church—Suppression of Monasteries—Alarming Discontents excited by the Court of Rome—Arrest and Suicide of Thaddeus Byrne—Insurrection of O'Neil and the Northern Chieftains—Battle of Bellahoe—Fleming Lord Slane—Recal and Execution of Lord Leonard Grey—Tragical Death of James Earl of Ormond—Activity of Sir William Brereton—Sir Anthony St. Leger, Lord Deputy—Henry VIII. proclaimed King of Ireland—Distinguished reception of the Irish Chieftains at Greenwich—New Civil and Ecclesiastical Regulations—Commercial Disputes between Limerick and Galway—Piracies of Sir Fineen O'Driscol—Destruction of Dunalong Castle by the Waterfordians—Extraordinary Escape of Lieutenant Grant—Introduction of Stage Plays into Ireland.. 106

CHAPTER VI.

Accession of Edward VI.—Insurrection of O'More and O'Connor—Sir Edward Bellingham, Lord Deputy—The Earl of Desmond reclaimed—Sir Anthony St. Leger, Lord Deputy—Efforts

CONTENTS.

PAGE

to establish the Reformation—Proclamation enjoining the new Liturgy—Opposition of Primate Dowdall—The Bible printed—Sir James Crofts, Lord Deputy—Conference of the Clergy at St. Mary's Abbey--Flight of Dowdall--Bale, Bishop of Ossory—Defeat of Sir James Crofts—Death of Edward VI.—Accession of Queen Mary—Gerald Earl of Kildare — Fitzmaurice Lord Kerry—Sir Anthony St. Leger, Lord Deputy—Ejection of the Protestant Clergy—Proceedings and suffering of Bishop Bale—A Jubilee—The Earl of Sussex, Lord Deputy—The Roman Catholic Worship restored—The Scotch expelled from Carrickfergus—Murder of Lord Dungannon — Hostilities between O'Neil and O'Donnel—Surprise and Defeat of John O'Neil—Death of O'Cahan—Story of Dean Cole..... 131

CHAPTER VII.

Accession of Elizabeth—John O'Neil assumes the Sovereignty of Ulster—His Interview with Sir Henry Sidney—Restoration of the Reformed Worship—Primate Loftus—Creagh, the titular Primate—Discontents—Insurrection in Ulster—John O'Neil in London—O'Neil restored to favour—The Geraldines and Butlers—Battle of Affane—Sir Henry Sidney, Lord Deputy—Mac Arthy More—Hostile proceedings of O'Neil—Battle of Derry—Destruction of Armagh—Battle of Dundalk — John O'Neil assassinated—Feuds in the South—Desmond arrested and sent

CONTENTS.

to the Tower of London—Vigorous conduct of Sir Henry Sidney—A Parliament—Attainder of John O'Neil...... 161

CHAPTER VIII.

Formation of New Counties—Insurrection of Sir Edmund Butler—Sir Peter Carew—Battle of Kilkenny—Outrages of James Fitzmaurice—Siege of Kilkenny—Siege of Cork—Sir John Perrot, President of Munster—Fitzmaurice's submission—Sir William Fitzwilliam, Lord Deputy—Plantations in Ulster—Sir Thomas Smith—Walter Earl of Essex—Hostilities with Bryan O'Neil—Escape of Desmond—Capture and Execution of Bryan O'Neil—Sir Henry Sidney, Lord Deputy—The Viceroy's Progress—Sir William Drury President of Munster—Action with the Desmonians near Tralee—Death of the Earl of Essex—Insurrection of the Mac-an-Eailas in Connaught—Grana-Uille............... 188

CHAPTER IX.

Traitorous proceedings of Stukely and Fitzmaurice—Sir William Drury, Lord Deputy—Spanish Debarkation at Smerwick—Sir John of Desmond—Murder of Henry Danvers—Death of Fitzmaurice—Duplicity of the Earl of Desmond—Action at Murrow—Battle of Manister—Sir William Pelham, Lord Deputy—Desmond and his Brother proclaimed Traitors—Capture and re-capture of Youghal—The Spaniards at Smer-

CONTENTS.

wick put to the sword—Capture and Execution of Sir James Desmond—Dreadful state of the Country.. 209

CHAPTER X.

Arthur Lord Grey, Lord Deputy—Battle of the Seven Churches—Death of Sir Francis Cosby—Dorcas Sidney—Battle of Stradbally Bridge—Death of Sir Alexander Cosby and his Son—Fresh arrival of Spaniards in the South—Repulse of the Earl of Ormond at Fort de l'Or—Sir Walter Raleigh—Capture of Fort de l'Or—Recal of Arthur Lord Grey—Exploits of Sir Walter Raleigh—Capture and Death of Sir John of Desmond—Sir John Perrot, Lord Deputy—Popularity of his Government—Scotch Invasion of Ulster repelled—A Parliament—Confiscation of Desmond's Lands—Plantation of Munster—Commotions in Connaught—Disputes between the Viceroy and Sir Richard Bingham—Defeat of De Bourgho................. 226

CHAPTER XI.

Discontents in Ulster—Character of Hugh O'Neil—He obtains the Earldom of Tyrone—Treacherous Seizure and Imprisonment of Red Hugh O'Donnel—Recal and Death of Sir John Perrot—Sir William Fitzwilliam, Lord Deputy—The Spanish Armada—Wrecks on the Irish coast—Kind reception of the Spaniards by the Natives O'Ruare and Don Antonio de Leva

CONTENTS.

—Avarice and cruelty of the Viceroy—Tyrone's Dissimulation—Escape and perilous Adventures of Red Hugh O'Donnel—Tyrone's Outrages—Sir William Russel, Lord Deputy—Maguire of Fermanagh—Action at Sciath-na-Fearth—Death of Archbishop Magawran—Exploits of O'Donnel—Siege of Enniskillen—Action at the Ford of Biscuits—Devastation of Connaught—Tyrone commences Hostilities—Sieges of Portmor and the Castle of Monaghan—Sir John Norris—Battle at the Pass of Cluain-Tibhin—Terrible Conflict between Tyrone and Sedgrave—Conference and Armistice with Tyrone and O'Donnel—Renewal of Hostilities—Action at Killoter—Capture of Armagh by a singular stratagem — Temporary submission of the Ulster Chieftains—Sir Conyers Clifford, President of Connaught—Death of Sir John Norris—Thomas Lord Borough, Lord Deputy—Fresh Hostilities—Defeat of Sir Conyers Clifford at Tyrrel's-Pass—Exploits of O'Donnel in Connaught—The Viceroy Defeats Tyrone near Armagh—Death of Lord Borough and the young Earl of Kildare—Tyrone's Conference with the Earl of Ormond—Sir Henry Bagnal marches to the relief of Portmor—Surprise of Tyrone's camp—Battle of the Yellow Ford—Death of Field Marshal Bagnal, and decisive Defeat of the Royal Army.. 253

CHAPTER XII.

Effects of Tyrone's Victory—Insurrection in Lein-

CONTENTS.

ster and Munster—The Sugan Earl of Desmond—Robert Earl of Essex, Lord Lieutenant——Action at the Pass of Plumes—Defeat of the Royal Forces by O'Byrne of Wicklow—Vigorous Hostilities of Red Hugh O'Donnel—Battle at the Curlew Mountains—Death of Sir Conyers Clifford—Conference between Essex and Tyrone—Discontent of the Queen and the English Council — Fall of Essex — Tyrone's Manifesto—His visit to Munster—Death of Sir Thomas Norris and Sir Warham St. Leger—Charles Lord Mountjoy, Lord Lieutenant—Sir George Carew, President of Munster—Vigor of the new Viceroy—Tyrone's escape into Ulster—Capture of the Earl of Ormond by Rory O'More—Sir Henry Dockwra captures Derry—Action at the Moyry pass—Insurrection in Leinster—Death of O'More—Affairs of Munster—Florence Mac Arthy—Action near Kinsale—The President's March to Limerick—Surrender of the Castle of Lough-Gur—Attempt of Dermod O'Connor to seize the titular Earl—Siege of Glin-Castle — Exploits of Maurice Stack—Capture of the Castle of Lixnaw—Murder of Maurice Stack—The Titular Earl a fugitive—Lord James Fitzgerald restored to the Earldom of Desmond—His reception at Kilmallock—Death of Dermod O'Connor—Sir Charles Wilmot—Siege of Listowel—Singular preservation of Lord Kerry's son—Submission of the Munster Rebels—Seizure of the titular Earl.... 301

CONTENTS.

CHAPTER XIII.

PAGE

Vigorous proceedings of Lord Mountjoy in Ulster —Action at Benburb— Landing of Spanish Troops at Kinsale, under Don Juan de Aquila —Advance of the Viceroy against the Invaders— Siege of Kinsale—March of Tyrone and O'Donnel to the South—Perilous state of the English army—Battle of Kinsale and Flight of the Irish Chieftains—Death of Red Hugh O'Donnel— Surrender of Kinsale—Obstinate Defence of the Castle of Dunboy—Death of M'Egan the Apostolic Vicar — Perilous Flight of O'Sullivan, O'Connor Kerry, &c. — Defeat and Death of Captain Malby—Singular preservation of O'Sullivan's Family—Story of Teig Keugh Mac Mahon and Henry O'Brien of Trummera—The Viceroy's Proceedings in Ulster—Final overthrow and Submission of Tyrone—Death of Queen Elizabeth.................................. 342

TRUE STORIES, &c.

IRELAND UNDER THE TUDORS.

CHAPTER I.

Accession of Henry VII.—Aversion of the Irish to his Government—Imposture of Lambert Simnel—He arrives in Dublin—The Lord Deputy Kildare proclaims him King, by the name of Edward VI.—General Defection of the Irish—Loyalty of Waterford—Intrigues of the Duchess of Burgundy—Arrival of Flemish Troops in Dublin—Coronation of Simnel—The Impostor invades England—Battle of Stoke—Capture and Degradation of the Mock King—Arrival of Sir Richard Edgecombe—Submission and Pardon of the Earl of Kildare—Feuds in Ulster.

I HAVE endeavoured, in the First Series of these Stories, to give you a brief view of the early history of Ireland, as far as the dim light of our ancient records would permit; and to narrate the commencement, and trace the growth of that singular connexion, which, for nearly seven centuries, has placed two neighbouring nations, differing widely in character, language, manners, and, for half that period, in religion, under the acknowledged dominion of the same sovereign. If you have perused the subject with attention, you must now be acquainted with those circumstances, some apparently fortuitous, and others arising from the political state of the country, which introduced the first English colony, and enabled them to maintain their ground in this island, in despite of the fierce but ill-conducted incursions of the natives, and the still more dangerous feuds of their own ambitious chieftains. The cruel and desultory warfare carried on in Ireland to the close of the reign of Edward IV. is, in a great measure, to be attributed to the lust of foreign conquest, by which nearly all the English monarchs had been actuated, previous to that period, and which necessarily weakened their efforts for the complete subjugation of the country. It was reserved for the House of Tudor to wrest their nominal sceptres from its ancient princes, and reduce the whole kingdom to an acknowledgment of English supremacy.

The crimes by which Richard III., the last monarch of the House of Plantagenet, mounted to power, can find few parallels in the annals of nations, fraught as they are with details of perfidy and blood. But the evil effects of Richard's enormities had not extended to Ireland; the attachment of its population to the house of York consequently remained undiminished, and the intelligence of a revolution which placed Henry VII., a prince of the hostile family on the throne, was received with feelings of popular discontent. Jasper earl of Pembroke, the king's uncle, was created, soon after Henry's coronation, duke of Bedford, and appointed lord lieutenant of Ireland; and to the astonishment of all parties, Gerald earl of Kildare was continued in his post of lord deputy; his brother Thomas, in that of lord chancellor; and all the other state officers, generally devoted Yorkists, were permitted to retain their places. It is probable that Henry was sufficiently aware of the unpopularity of his family in this country to attempt any change in its government, till his throne was better established, and especially as the earl of Ormond, one of his most powerful adherents, had lost much of his influence in Ireland, by a long residence at the English court.

Henry's marriage with the heiress of the house of York, was calculated to conciliate the affections of his Irish subjects; but the coldness with which he treated his bride, his cruel and unnecessary imprisonment of the young earl of Warwick, the son of their favorite Clarence, and the numerous attainders and forfeitures with which the friends of the house of York were visited in England, rekindled in their minds the flames of discontent, and the majority of the nation ardently panted for some new revolution, to subvert a government which they detested. Circumstances soon occurred, which for a season, elevated their hopes. In 1486, lord Lovel and Sir Humphry Stafford levied a body of forces in the north of England; but this attempt at insurrection terminated in the execution of Stafford, and the flight of Lovel to the court of Margaret, duchess of Burgundy, sister of Edward IV., where for some time he found ample employment in assisting to mature a conspiracy against Henry's government, as singular for its contrivance, its temporary success, and termination, as any to be found in the fables of romance.

The design of raising up a pretender to the crown of England is said to have originated with one Richard Simon, a priest, at Oxford; but it is generally believed that he did not attempt the accomplishment of his plan without the knowledge and sanction of the queen dowager, who now finding that her services in contributing to Henry's elevation, were only rewarded by neglect and cruelty to herself and her family, had conceived the most violent animosity against him. It is therefore considered probable that she would, under these feelings, lend her sanction to any feasible attempt to subvert his government, knowing that, this once accomplished, the impostor could be easily set aside. There lived at that time in Oxford, a youth named Lambert Simnel, the son of a baker, who possessed an understanding above his years, (which were only fifteen,) manners greatly superior to his rank in life, and the air and deportment of a person of illustrious birth. This youth was fixed on by Simon as the chief actor in his scheme of imposture. He entertained him at his house, flattered his inexperience, taught him those lessons which were necessary for the exalted character which he was about to assume; 'and a report having been at this time industriously spread, that Richard, the younger son of Edward IV. had secretly escaped from the cruelty of his uncle, it was at first intended that Simnel should personate that prince. A difficulty, however, presented itself to this scheme, as the young duke of York, if alive, would now be only twelve years old. A fresh report was therefore circulated, that the earl of Warwick had just escaped from the Tower, and it was finally decided that Simnel should personate that unhappy prince.

Except that his age agreed more nearly with

that of Warwick, this new plan was attended with still greater difficulties than the former; as the duke of York, being a child in the nursery at the time of his father's death, was known to few, while the son of Clarence had appeared at Edward's court, and had been on the most intimate terms with many of the nobility. But to obviate the consequences of too close an inspection, it was resolved to commence the project at a distance from the court, and amongst a people whose prepossessions in favour of the house of York would not allow them to be over scrupulous in their examination of the pretender's claims. To qualify him for the execution of his part of this singular drama, Simnel was made acquainted with all the adventures of the earl of Warwick, and accurately instructed to converse with ease on various persons and incidents, information which he must have derived from those of higher rank than his ecclesiastical preceptor.

The jealous and vigilant monarch was soon apprised that some plan for disturbing the tranquillity of his government was in agitation, and his first suspicions were directed against the earl of Kildare, as a person from whom the greatest danger was to be apprehended. Henry was fully aware of the aversion of the Irish to his government, and he issued a summons to the earl to repair to his court, under pretence of consulting him respecting the affairs of that country. But Kildare, apprehensive that his correspondence with the malcontents of England had been discovered, and possessing too much prudence to place his life or liberty in the hands of a severe and vindictive prince, prevailed on some of the chief lords and prelates to sign a memorial to his majesty, stating that the deputy's departure might prove highly prejudicial to some affairs of the greatest importance which were then in progress through parliament, and praying that his majesty would recal, or at least suspend his mandate until these weighty matters were decided. Thus powerfully supported, Kildare ventured to postpone his voyage to England; and the critical situation of affairs compelled Henry to acquiesce in his reasons.

The arrival of Simnel with his preceptor in Dublin, soon put an end to all doubt on the subject. This event was speedily notified to the lord deputy, who granted the impostor and his wily instructor a private audience, at which Simnel, in all the dignity of an injured prince, proclaimed himself to be the son of the unfortunate Clarence, traced his pedigree with the strictest accuracy, related in the most pathetic language the particulars of his imprisonment, his escape, and the hardships which he had since endured ; inveighed with well-affected passion against the usurpation of the earl of Richmond, and finally demanded the protection of the lord deputy for the rightful heir to the crown of England. Kildare listened to this tale with profound attention, commiserated all his wrongs, and sending for his brother the chancellor, and lord Portlester the treasurer, introduced Simnel to them as the last hope of the house of York, to which they were both ardently devoted. They received the adventurer with the warmest expressions of zealous attachment; but before they proceeded further in the business, they resolved to try the temper of the people by circulating far and near, that the earl of Warwick, the son of their much-loved countryman, Clarence, had arrived in Dublin. The intelligence produced the most extraordinary effects, not only in the capital, but throughout the country. The citizens, as with one voice, declared in favour of the pretender, and forgetful that the female issue of Edward IV. had prior claims, indulged the vain hope of giving as a king to England the son of a man who had drawn his first breath amongst them.

The whole nation now declared for the pretender, with the exception of the citizens of Waterford, Octavian de Palatio the primate, who was an Italian; the prelates of Cashel, Tuam, Clogher, and Ossory; the Butler and Bermingham families, and the baron of Howth. Encouraged by such powerful support, Kildare assembled the council, who giving their cordial assent to Simnel's claim, the mock monarch was conveyed in triumph to the castle of Dublin, and proclaimed king by the name of Edward VI. The example of the metropolis was followed by all the principal cities of Ireland, except Waterford, against which the vengeance of the lord deputy was speedily denounced.

Kildare despatched a messenger to that city, peremptorily commanding John Butler, the mayor, to proclaim the new king, and to receive and assist him with all his forces. Butler sent a written reply by a courier of his own, in which he informed the earl, that the citizens of Waterford considered him and all who had assisted him in proclaiming the impostor Simnel, as rebels to the rightful king of England. Enraged at the boldness of this reply, Kildare ordered the messenger to be hanged, and sent a herald to Waterford, clad in his coat of arms, to deliver another message to the citizens, who commanded them and their mayor to proclaim the new king, and accept him as their rightful prince, under pain of hanging at their own doors. Butler valorously replied that he would not give the deputy the trouble to come and hang him at his door, but, God willing, he would march out with his citizens, aided by the inhabitants of Clonmel, Fethard, and Callan, to encounter the false king and his adherents thirty miles from Waterford; and, he doubted not, would give them an overthrow, to their dishonour and infamy. The lord deputy not having it in his power immediately to avenge this insult, contented himself with uttering some additional threats, and declaring the possessions and franchises of the refractory city forfeited.

When king Henry received intelligence of these proceedings from his friends in Ireland, he adopted the most vigorous means to counteract the plans of his enemies. The queen dowager, whom he strongly suspected as a principal agent in the conspiracy, was seized and committed to a nunnery; and to prevent the infatuation of his Irish subjects from becoming contagious in England, he took the real earl of Warwick from the Tower, and had him conveyed in procession through the streets of the metropolis to St. Paul's church, where he was exhibited to an immense concourse of spectators. But however this might have satisfied the people of London with regard to Simnel's imposture, it produced no change in the opinions or conduct of the Yorkists in Ireland, who boldly retorted the charge of imposture on the usurper, as they called him; alleging that he had "imposed on public credulity by exhibiting a mock prince, tricked out in the form of the real Plantagenet; and they endeavoured by numerous emissaries to circulate these opinions amongst the people of England. They at the same time sent trusty messengers to the duchess of Burgundy, a princess who was rich and powerful, possessed of a bold and masculine spirit, and at this time filled with indignation against Henry, on account of his unremitting severities against the partisans of her family. They informed her of all the late transactions in Ireland, and implored her aid as the sovereign patroness of an enterprize in behalf of her persecuted nephew, to which, they said, Providence had already granted the most miraculous success. The court of Burgundy was at this period the residence of several of the English malcontents, amongst whom was John de la Pole, earl of Lincoln, a nephew of Edward IV. whom the usurper Richard had destined to be his successor, if he should die without issue. He therefore fully entered into the views of his aunt with regard to the Irish adventure, knowing that if by means of Simnel, he could dethrone king Henry, the instrument could be easily disposed of. It was now resolved that the most prompt measures should be adopted to aid the cause of the impostor, and early in 1487, two thousand veteran troops were despatched to Ireland, under the command of Swaart, an experienced leader, who was accompanied by the earl of Lincoln, lord Lovel, and some other English Yorkists.

Encouraged by the arrival of these succours in Dublin, the Yorkists exulted as if the triumph of their cause were already completed; and Kildare, with his council, resolved to crown the puppet-king with all the magnificence that circumstances would permit. Simnel, clad in royal robes, was conducted in great pomp to the cathedral of Christ's church, attended by the lord-deputy, his state officers, and all the English and Irish nobles then in the metropolis. Pain, the bishop of Meath, enforced his right to the throne in an elaborate discourse from the pulpit; and Fitz-simons, the archbishop of Dublin, completed the ceremony by placing on his head a rich diadem, which had long adorned an image of the Virgin in St. Mary's abbey. The church was filled with the acclamations of the delighted spectators, and the spectacle was concluded, according to the ancient Irish custom, by the newly-crowned king being carried on the shoulders of Darcy of Platten, the chief of a powerful English family in Meath, to the castle of Dublin—where he instantly commenced the exercise of royal authority. Various acts of council were passed in his name, and a parliament was summoned, by which laws were enacted, subsidies granted, and forfeitures and attainders denounced against the city of Waterford, the family of Butler, and others, who were declared to be rebellious and refractory subjects.

The administration of the Irish government was thus, for a few weeks, carried on in the name of Edward VI. probably with the view of provoking Henry to head an expedition into this country. But that prince was too sagacious rashly to abandon the seat of his government to the machinations of his English enemies, and he contented himself with guarding the coasts both of Ireland and Flanders, to prevent fresh supplies from being conveyed to the malcontents, and procuring the spiritual thunders of the see of Rome against all the opposers of his royal rights.

While the Anglo-Irish were thus actively engaged in supporting what they pretended to be the interest of the house of York, the native chieftains, regardless of the power of either party, pursued their predatory career on the borders of the Pale, and the partisans of the new king soon perceived that it would be impossible to realize their dream of royalty in a country where the resources were inadequate to support the ordinary establishment of the state, much less a numerous army. It therefore became obviously necessary to change the scene of operations, and all parties agreed that the contest for the crown must be decided on English ground. The veteran Flemings under Swaart were fully prepared for action, and their ranks were soon swelled by thousands of gallant Irish, led on by the lords Thomas and Maurice Fitzgerald, brothers of the lord deputy. The earl of Lincoln assumed the command of this expedition, which embarked with the most sanguine hopes of success. Arrived at Foudrey in Lancashire, they exultingly exhibited their young king, whose right to the throne they called on all the Yorkists of England to vindicate.

Henry was not unprepared for this event. He took all the necessary precautions in those counties which he most suspected, for repelling the invasion; and having made a judicious disposition of his forces, he with great appearance of devotion visited the shrine of our Lady of Walsingham, and from thence continued his progress to the menaced districts in the north of England. The earl of Lincoln having been joined at his landing by Sir Thomas Broughton with some forces, imprudently directed his march towards York, where Henry had so lately triumphed over lord Lovel. His army every where maintained the strictest order, as if to show the anxiety of the young king for the peace and welfare of his subjects; but the people viewed its progress with silent astonishment, and Lincoln soon perceived that a decisive victory could alone ensure the success of the

BATTLE OF STOKE.

enterprise. He accordingly advanced to surprise the town of Newark, but king Henry interposing his army between the rebels and the town, a battle became inevitable.

On the 20th of June, 1487, the two armies met at the village of Stoke, in the county of Nottingham, and an engagement ensued of the most sanguinary description. The king's forces were superior both in number and quality; yet the furious valour of the Irish, aided by the experience of Swaart and his veteran Germans, kept the victory doubtful for a considerable time. But in the end the light armour of the Irish proved unavailing against the efforts of the royal army, and the number of their German auxiliaries was insufficient to resist their overwhelming charge: yet though broken they disdained to fly, and fell in heaps under the stroke of the victors. The earl of Lincoln, lords Thomas and Maurice Fitzgerald, with Plunket, and many other Irishmen of distinction, the brave Swaart and Sir Thomas Broughton, all fell on the field of battle, with four thousand of their unhappy followers. Lord Lovel having been never afterwards heard of, is supposed to have shared a similar fate. Simnel, with Simon his tutor, fell into the hands of king Henry, who, with an affected magnanimity, abstained from taking sanguinary vengeance on such ignoble captives. He ordered Simon to be immured in a dungeon for life, and assigned to Simnel a menial office in his own kitchen, from which he was afterwards promoted to the rank of falconer to his majesty —a post superior, perhaps, to what he would have attained, had he never engaged in this singular enterprise.

This treasonable attempt having been thus speedily suppressed, it might reasonably be expected that a prince of Henry's vindictive temper would at once hurl his vengeance against its Irish abettors. But his policy always kept his views of strict justice within due bounds; and he contented himself for the present with issuing a letter to the citizens of Waterford, in which he applauded their loyal opposition to Kildare and the citizens of Dublin, and procuring a papal bull against those prelates and other delinquent clergy who had embraced the cause of Simnel. The mayor and citizens of

Waterford were at the same time armed with full power to seize all rebels by sea or land. From these proceedings Kildare and his partisans perceived that a storm of vengeance was collecting against them, which they allayed by a timely submission, endeavouring to palliate their fault, imploring his majesty's pardon, and promising to atone for their error by their future good conduct. The still distracted state of England induced Henry to receive this submission, and Kildare was continued in his government, with the hint that the royal grace must depend upon his future dutiful and loyal conduct.

Henry, still suspicious of the fidelity of his Irish subjects, sent, in the summer of 1488, Sir Richard Edgecombe to Ireland, with a body of five hundred men, to compel the great lords to renew their oaths of allegiance, and offer the king's pardon to all who would give assurance of their future loyalty. Sir Richard arrived at Kinsale on the 27th of June, and in the church received the homage of the lords Barry and Courcey, and the townsmen swore allegiance to king Henry VII. From thence he proceeded in a coasting voyage to Waterford, where he was honorably received and lodged in the house of Butler the mayor, who had in the preceding year so vigorously withstood the threats of the earl of Kildare, and who now accompanied Sir Richard Edgecombe through the city, and entreated that if the earl were again restored to his power and dignity, Waterford might be exempt from his jurisdiction, and hold immediately of the king and his heirs. Sir Richard after expressing his royal master's high commendation of the truth and loyalty of the citizens of Waterford, offered his services with the king in their behalf; and having partaken of an entertainment with the mayor, he returned to his ships, and arrived in the harbour of Dublin on the 3d of July.

The bishop of Meath, with the clergy and magistrates of the capital received the king's commissioner with the most respectful submission; but the haughty Kildare, having by this time recovered from his first panic, absented himself under the pretence of being engaged on a pilgrimage, and seven days elapsed before he consented to an interview with Edgecombe.

The lord deputy was received with a severity which he returned with cold civility; and after considerable discussion, he was allowed to dictate the terms on which he would accept his pardon. Homage and fealty were then performed by the earl of Kildare, the lords Portlester, Gormanston, Slane, Trimblestone, and Dunsany, with the prelates of Dublin, Meath, and Kildare, and some abbots and priors; and they were immediately absolved from the pope's sentence of excommunication: but so apprehensive was the English commissioner of prevarication on the part of the Anglo-Irish lords, that the host on which they were sworn was, by stipulation, consecrated by a chaplain of his own. What a picture of the state of society at that period, does this circumstance afford us!

As during the late revolt, the outrages of the native Irish had greatly increased, Henry found it necessary to continue the earl of Kildare in the government, as the only person in the island who possessed sufficient vigour and influence to repel their incursions. This excited the jealousy of those who had evinced their loyalty to the reigning sovereign during the general defection, and Octavian the primate, earnestly sought the office of chancellor as a counterbalance to the enormous power of the deputy. Kildare, to overthrow his project, sent Pain, the bishop of Meath to the king, who, unable to decide between the conflicting parties, summoned the earl and the other principal Irish lords to his presence. They soon after attended him at Greenwich, where Henry invited them to a banquet, at which Lambert Simnel, to whom they had so lately bowed the knee as their sovereign, officiated in the capacity of butler; but the king followed up this rebuke of their folly by a confirmation of their pardon. Kildare and his friends were continued in their offices, and obtained the most gracious assurances of his majesty's favour and confidence.

The lord deputy conducted his government for many years with such vigour and success, as to obtain the title in future ages of the great earl. The favour shown to him by his sovereign, silenced, for some time, the clamours of his rivals, while he crushed every attempt of the Irish chieftains to disturb the English settlements, either by the sword, or the influence which he had acquired over the minds of the natives.* But he failed in his efforts to extinguish a bloody feud which broke out in Ulster, in the year 1491, between his kinsman, Con O'Neil, and Hugh O'Donnel, the powerful chieftain of Tyrconnel, now called Donegal. The quarrel originated in O'Donnel's refusing to pay tribute or head-rent to O'Neil, as his liege lord. The demand was reiterated by the latter in the following laconic style, '*Pay me my rent, or if you dont*——,' and a reply was returned by O'Donnel of equal strength and brevity, '*I owe you no rent, and if I did*——.' This being sufficient to rouse their fiery spirits, a sanguinary conflict ensued, which continued with various success, till O'Neil was murdered by his own brother in January, 1492.

* The first muskets seen in Ireland were sent as a present from Germany to this lord deputy in 1489, and were from this time borne by his guard before his residence in Thomas-court.

CHAPTER II.

Pretensions of Perkin Warbeck to the Crown of England—Kildare removed from Office—Walter Archbishop of Dublin, Lord Deputy—Perkin Warbeck at Cork—Maurice (Bellicosus) Earl of Desmond—Perkin retires to France—The Sweating Sickness—The Archbishop of Dublin's Interview with King Henry—Memorial on the miserable State of Ireland—Sir Edward Poynings appointed Lord Deputy—O'Hanlon's Insurrection—Kildare suspected—Poynings' Parliament—Attainder of Kildare—Return of Perkin Warbeck—Siege of Waterford—Repulse of Warbeck and the Earl of Desmond—Subsequent Adventures and Death of Perkin Warbeck—Kildare committed to the Tower—Kildare and the Bishop of Meath before the King—Kildare's Singular Triumph—Murder of Lord Barry.

THE restless duchess of Burgundy raised up, about this time, another pretender to the throne of England, in the person of Perkin Warbeck. This youth is said to have been born in London, of Jewish parents, who afterwards settled at Tournay in Flanders; and possessing, like Simnel, the qualifications for the part which he was destined to act, he was instructed in all things necessary to sustain the character of Richard duke of York, the youngest son of Edward IV. who it was still pretended had escaped from the Tower. Ireland being also selected for the first appearance of this new adventurer, emissaries were sent there to prepare the minds of the Yorkists for his reception, while Warbeck retired to Portugal till a favourable opportunity presented itself for the commencement of his enterprise.

The vigilant Henry having received intimation of those proceedings from his friends in Ireland, became apprehensive of the fidelity of the principal abettors of Simnel, whom his policy had led him to continue in power. He resolved, therefore, at every risk, to remove Kildare and Portlester from the administration; and in the month of October, 1492, Walter

Fitz-simmons, archbishop of Dublin, was appointed lord deputy; Plunket, the chief justice, was nominated lord chancellor; and the office of treasurer was conferred on Sir James Ormond. Kildare was terribly provoked by his sudden removal from office, and particularly as it led to the restoration to power of his ancient rivals the Butlers. The chief of their house was at present in high favour with the king, who had lately sent him on an important embassy to the court of France; and the arrival of Sir James, who might be considered his representative, caused the long-smothered animosities of the rival families to burst into a flame. The Geraldines and Butlers once more flew to arms, and their respective territories became for some time a scene of murder and devastation.

The new deputy, in the mean time, assembled a parliament, in which the conduct of Kildare and Portlester was condemned with the greatest severity, and all the late measures against the Butlers and the citizens of Waterford were revoked. In the midst of these proceedings, Perkin Warbeck landed at Cork, without troops or retinue, and declared himself to be Richard Plantagenet, who had escaped from the Tower. He was received by John Walters, the mayor, and the principal citizens, with all the honours due to a sovereign prince, and immediately despatched letters to the earls of Kildare and Desmond, notifying his arrival, and acknowledging the loyal attachment and zealous services of those noblemen to the house of York. It does not appear in what manner Kildare received these overtures; but Desmond instantly declared in his favour. The southern branch of the Geraldines had, after the decapitation of Earl Thomas, in 1467, continued for many years in a state of comparative tranquillity. His son James, who does not appear to have inherited the ambition of his house, was murdered in 1487 by his own servants, at Court-Mattress, in the county of Limerick. He was succeeded by his brother Maurice, who, though so lame as to be always carried in a horse-litter, displayed such a warlike propensity that he acquired the surname of *Bellicosus*. After avenging the death of his brother, he turned his arms against O'Carrol and M'Arthy, the chieftains of Ely and Cork; and elated by his victories over them, he now cheerfully embarked in an enterprize which he hoped would lead to the dethronement of the sovereign of England.

But as Perkin was not yet prepared to commence his operations, his visit appears to have been intended only to revive the dormant zeal of the Yorkists, and keep their hopes alive till his plans were brought to maturity. After a short residence in Cork, he repaired to France, where Charles VIII. gave him royal entertainment, and he was speedily joined by above one hundred English gentlemen. During the three following years he resided at the court of the duchess of Burgundy, who openly acknowledged him as her nephew. The transient appearance of the adventurer in Ireland had produced the intended effect. The court of England was filled with endless accusations from a wretched country, where the spirit of faction was again let loose, and where the unhappy population were suffering under all the horrors of famine, and of a terrible disease, called the *sweating sickness,* by which multitudes perished in every part of the kingdom. Its symptoms were acute pain in the head, a burning heat in the stomach, intense thirst, and a profuse perspiration of fetid matter. It seized chiefly on young and middle-aged men, who, if they did not resist the first impulse to sleep, inevitably died.

The distracted and miserable state of the country at length excited the attention of the English monarch, who commanded archbishop Walter, the deputy, to repair to London, and lay before him a full detail of all the circumstances of the Irish government. On his arrival at court, the piety and gravity of the prelate of Dublin caused him to be received with particular attention. When Henry inquired of him, why his Irish subjects were so prone to faction and rebellion? the archbishop replied, with the simplicity of an ecclesiastic, that it was to be attributed chiefly to the idle manner in which the younger sons of rich families spent their time—who, instead of qualifying themselves for trade or a liberal profession, lived in a state of dependence on the head of the family, and so became useless to the commonwealth;

while the common people lived in sloth and indolence, on account of the great plenty of provisions that the land naturally produced. This was certainly one cause of the disorders in Ireland; but a memorial was about this time presented to King Henry, which took a more extended view of the subject—the author's object appearing to be, to engage the king in a complete reduction and settlement of the country. He enumerated no less than sixty regions still governed by Irish chieftains after their ancient laws and manners, and a long catalogue of degenerate English, who refused all obedience to government. The English pale comprised only half the counties of Uriel (Louth,) Meath, Kildare, Dublin, and Wexford; and even in these the common people entirely conformed to the Irish habits, manners, and language. The country was universally harassed by oppressive exactions, unnatural feuds, and expeditions undertaken by deputies from personal animosity, without any benefit to the state—the necessary consequence was, that the laws were neglected or defied, while an universal ignorance prevailed, from the scandalous neglect of instructing and reforming the people. To remedy these evils, the king was exhorted to appoint a chief governor of ability and integrity, supported by a military force sufficient to restrain the Irish enemy, and put an end to local feuds, and thus gradually reduce the whole body of the inhabitants to obedience; and to substitute a system of equitable and moderate taxation for those arbitrary impositions by which the people in many districts had been almost impoverished.

This memorial is supposed to have had considerable influence on the king's subsequent designs with regard to Ireland, as he resolved immediately to adopt many of the measures which it suggested. In the mean time, Kildare had repaired to the English court to defend himself against the accusations which he suspected archbishop Walter had laid against him; but the prelate and the partisans of Ormond had now so completely prepossessed the mind of the king against the late lord deputy, that he refused to hear his defence, referring it to the decision of Sir Edward Poynings, an English knight, in whom he placed peculiar confidence, and whom he was now about to entrust with the Irish government, armed with sufficient powers to punish the delinquent and reward the meritorious. In September, 1494, the new viceroy arrived in Ireland, with a force of about a thousand troops, and nearly all the state-officers and judges were replaced by Englishmen.

Poynings soon commenced energetic measures to break the power of the great lords who had hitherto encouraged factions amongst their followers, and, when in power, modelled the parliament according to their will. Previous to attempting any extension of the English authority amongst the old natives, he determined on reforming the Pale, and putting an end to those oppressions by which the king's subjects were so dreadfully harassed. But, before he could take any effective step towards the accomplishment of these desirable objects, the long-continued and dangerous insurrection of O'Hanlon, an Irish chieftain of Ulster, compelled him to march into that province at the head of a considerable military force. He was accompanied in this expedition by Sir James Ormond and the earl of Kildare, who appeared anxious thus to efface the former suspicions of his loyalty. No glory attended an enterprise against an enemy who, instead of marching to meet their adversaries in all the pomp of chivalry, darted unexpectedly upon them from inaccessible woods and morasses, and became invisible at the approach of the royal army. Poynings could, therefore, find no opportunity to strike a decisive blow, and the enemies of Kildare seized this as a favourable moment for exciting his suspicions of the fidelity of that nobleman, whom they accused of holding a correspondence with the enemy, and actually conspiring with him to murder the king's deputy. These suggestions were in a great measure confirmed by the arrival of intelligence, that lord James Fitzgerald, the brother of Kildare, had taken possession of the castle of Carlow, in defiance of the royal authority. This afforded Poynings a pretext for withdrawing from the North; and marching to Carlow, he laid siege to the castle which surrendered after a week's resistance. The ill success of his first military expedition was wholly attributed by the deputy to the traitorous practices of the Kildare family.

In the first week of December, 1494, Sir Edward Poynings assembled, at Drogheda, that famous parliament, whose regulations first gave to the Anglo-Irish any thing like a regular government; and which, during nearly three subsequent centuries, were referred to as forming a component part of the political constitution of Ireland. It is necessary that you should be made acquainted with the nature of those enactments, as they exhibit in a striking point of view the previous miserable state of the country. The practice of *coyne* and *livery*, by which the people hitherto were compelled to pay and maintain the soldiers of their lords, was completely abolished, and in its place a moderate tax was substituted. To circumscribe further the power of these chieftains, it was ordained that no citizen, or freeman of any city should receive or pay wages as the retainer of any great lords, who were forbidden to retain any followers but their household officers and servants, except those who were necessary to defend the marches or borders. These lords were prohibited from becoming freemen or magistrates of any corporate towns, and from making war or peace without the consent of the deputy—they were also forbidden the use of fire arms without special license; the lower orders were strictly enjoined the regular use of archery; and the military cries and words of distinction among the several factions were declared to be seditious and illegal. The crime of murder which had hitherto, according to the Irish custom, been punished by a fine, was now declared to be high treason; and all the statutes passed at Kilkenny in the reign of Edward III. were confirmed, except that which prohibited the use of the Irish language and some others of minor importance. Various alterations were, at the same time made, in the mode of appointing state officers, and in consequence of many alleged abuses of authority, the judges were no longer to hold their places by patent for life, but during the king's pleasure. But the most memorable act of this parliament was that which has ever since been emphatically denominated ' Poynings' Law,' by which the right of the king's deputies to call a parliament at their pleasure was taken away, and it was ordained that " no parliament shall for the future be called in Ireland, until the chief governor shall have first certified to the king, as well of the causes and considerations of the acts which they design to pass, as of the acts themselves; and till the same shall be approved of by the king and council, and a license therefrom issued to summon a parliament." This act continued to regulate the parliamentary proceedings in Ireland till its legislative independence was asserted in 1782.

The enemies of Kildare being triumphant in this assembly, that great nobleman with all his kinsmen and adherents were declared attainted of high treason; and though his past conduct gave just ground of suspicion, the irritation of his kindred at the disgrace of their chief, soon hurried them into excesses which were readily imputed to his influence. In 1495, Perkin Warbeck with six hundred men had made an attempt on the coast of England, which was defeated, with the loss of one hundred and sixty of his followers. From thence he repaired once more to Cork, where he was cordially received by his old friends, and speedily joined by the earl of Desmond and lord Barry, at the head of a well appointed force of two thousand four hundred men. The first object of the confederates was to take vengeance on the refractory city of Waterford, whither they marched to invest it by land, while a fleet of eleven ships was directed to proceed to the little port of Passage, to attack it from the river. The citizens, apprized of their approach, resolved to maintain the loyal character which they had gained; and, besides various other means of defence, they raised a mound of earth to stop the course of the river, which filled the ponds of Kilbarry, an extensive marsh that protected the city on the south.

A party having landed from the ships near Lombard's Marsh, were speedily repulsed by the garrison, with considerable loss; and during the eleven days of the siege, several successful sorties were made, in which many of the enemy fell; and to such a pitch of cruel enthusiasm did the citizens carry their loyalty, that every unfortunate prisoner who fell into their hands, had his head chopped off in the market-place, and fastened on a stake in sight of the enemy. A cannon placed on Reginald's

Tower having by a lucky shot struck one of the ships, by which all the crew perished, Perkin and his friends became at length convinced of the futility of their enterprize, and abandoning the siege returned to Cork, while the victorious Waterfordians, commanded by Butler, their mayor, pursued the rebel fleet with four gallant ships to the mouth of that harbour. The adventurer, however, reached Kinsale in safety, from whence he sailed for Cornwall, and soon after took refuge in Scotland, where the king acknowledged his title to the crown of England, entered into an alliance with him, and gave him the lady Catherine Gordon, his relative, in marriage. These circumstances, with many others connected with the singular story of Perkin Warbeck, have excited strong doubts, whether this aspirer to the throne of England was an impostor; but of this as well as of many other secrets in our history mankind will probably remain ignorant to the end of time. The king of Scotland not only acknowledged his rights, but put himself at the head of an army to support them, with which he made a fruitless expedition into Northumberland in 1497. An insurrection in Cornwall in the following year, encouraged Warbeck to make a fresh effort, and having effected a landing at Whitsand-bay, he soon found himself at the head of several thousand men : but failing in an attempt on the city of Exeter, his army dispersed, and the unhappy youth with a few of his followers took refuge in the abbey of Beaulieu. He was induced soon after to surrender, on a promise that his life should be spared. Having, however, in the following year, formed a plan of escape, in which the unfortunate earl of Warwick was implicated, king Henry seized the opportunity of ridding himself of these dangerous rivals, and they were publicly executed, together with Walters, the mayor of Cork, who had been Warbeck's first abettor in Ireland.

In the mean time the earl of Kildare, on whom strong suspicion rested of having favored the late consiracy, was sent to London as a prisoner, while Poynings, to whose dispositions its defeat was attributed, returned to England in a kind of triumph, and was rewarded with the order of the Garter. The services of the citizens of Waterford were warmly acknowledged by the king in a letter to the mayor, and permission was granted them to use as the motto of the city arms—*Urbs intacta manet Waterfordia.*

The enemies of the Geraldines being now completely triumphant, Kildare was kept a close prisoner for more than a year, during which his countess, a daughter of lord Portlester, died of grief. But king Henry, in the interval, perceived that the earl was a man of an open temper and of unrefined and simple manners, rather than a cunning intriguer or dark conspirator; and that the crimes charged against him were only such as were likely to take place in a country so torn by turbulence and faction as Ireland had lately been: he, therefore, resolved to confront his captive with his adversaries, and thus give him a fair opportunity of defending himself. When the day of trial came, Creagh archbishop of Cashel, and Pain the bishop of Meath, stood forth as his principal accusers. The earl, at first appeared unable to answer to a charge brought against him by the bishop of Meath, that after Plunket and his followers had been slain by him in an action near Trim, he followed the bishop into a church with a drawn sword, and dragged him from his sanctuary. The king, perceiving his noble prisoner perplexed, gave him his choice of any counsel in England, and time to prepare his defence: "Grant me that," said the earl, "and I will answer to-morrow; but I doubt I shall not be allowed that good fellow I would choose." The king gave him his hand in assurance that he should, and his majesty asking him when he should choose his counsellor, "Never," cried the bishop, "if it be left to his choice." "Thou liest, *Bralagh*, bald bishop," retorted Kildare angrily, "as soon as thou wouldst choose to break thy vow of chastity, and that would be within an hour." The king and his lords were convulsed with laughter, at this uncourtly charge against the ecclesiastic, and Henry asked Kildare, if he said true? "By your hand," replied the earl, laying hold of the king's hand, "there is not in London a better mutton-master (glutton) or a more incontinent person, than yon shorn priest is. I know him well enough, and have three tales to tell your majesty of him, that I dare swear will make every body present laugh. I will now tell you a tale of this vicious prelate." Of the story we have no particulars, but during its narration the king and his courtiers were ready to burst with laughter, while the earl never changed countenance, but related it with as much unconcern, as if he were in the midst of his companions in his own country. When he had concluded, the king anxious to divert the discourse from the unfortunate bishop, thus made an object of ridicule, cautioned the earl to be well advised whom he would choose for his counsellor, for that whoever he should be, would have enough to do to defend him. "Marry," said Kildare, "I can see no better man in England than your majesty, and will choose no other." "By St. Brigid," said the king, "it was well chosen; for I thought your tale would not excuse your doings." "Do you think I am a fool," answered the earl, "no, I am a man both in the field and the town." Henry laughed, and said, that "a wiser man might have chosen worse." A new accusation was now brought forward, that in one of his lawless excursions he had burned the cathedral of Cashel to the ground. " Spare your evidence," said Kildare, " I did set fire to the church, for I thought the archbishop had been in it." This singular simplicity in pleading a circumstance of aggravation as an apology for his offence, threw an air of ridicule on his prosecutors which proved highly favorable to the cause of the accused; and when they concluded their charges by exclaiming passionately, " All Ireland cannot govern this earl!" " Well," replied the king, " this earl shall govern all Ireland."

The conduct of a prince of Henry's jealous and vindictive temper, in thus favouring Kildare may appear extraordinary; but it proves that he believed the late deputy had been imposed upon in the affair of Lambert Simnel; and that in the present state of Ireland, he conceived a nobleman of his vigorous, yet artless character, was the fittest person to be entrusted with the government of the country. He now gave him his fullest confidence, created him a Knight of the Garter, and restored him to all his estates and honors; and, at his request, granted patents of pardon to Desmond and all his adherents, with the exception of lord Barry, who was soon after murdered in his place of concealment by his unnatural brother David, the archdeacon of Cork. But the base act was speedily avenged by another branch of the family, and the body of the fratricide was burned by command of the earl of Desmond.

CHAPTER III.

Commotions in Ulster—Kildare restored to the office of Lord Deputy—His vigour and success—Interview between Kildare and Sir James Ormond at St. Patrick's Cathedral—Battle of Knocktuadh—Nugent Lord Delvin—Defeat of the Bourkes—Capture of Galway—Extraordinary instance of Civic Justice exemplified in the Story of Lynch, Mayor of Galway—Death and Character of Henry VII.

DURING the transactions recorded in the last chapter, Ireland continued a prey to civil warfare. Since the departure of Sir Edward Poynings, the government had been committed to the bishop of Bangor and Nugent lord Delvin, who with difficulty repressed the incursions of O'Brien, lord of Thomond, into the English settlements in the South, while in the Northern province, the close connexion which the Irish chieftains maintained with Scotland, rendered them a constant cause of alarm to the country. The sons of Con O'Neil had taken ample vengeance on his murderer Henry; and Neil Mac Art O'Neil, a partisan of the latter, retaliated by ravaging Armagh, Tyrone, and some other districts. King Henry finding his authority insufficient to quell these insurgents, called the papal thunders to his aid; but these proving equally inefficacious, he resolved once more to entrust the reins of the Irish government to the vigorous arm of Kildare, who had now become sincerely attached to the English interests by the recent instance of his sovereign's kind protection against his inveterate enemies, and this the lord deputy so fully evinced in all his after conduct, that his name became terrible to the insurgents. He marched rapidly into Ulster, where being joined by O'Donnel, Maguire, and Turlogh O'Neil, he seized the forts of Dungannon and Omagh, and in a few days reduced Mac Art to obedience. He now turned his attention to the South, where he acted with similar vigour, and placed garrisons in Cork and Kinsale to crush the remnant of disaffection which still existed amongst the inhabitants. He also appeared anxious to strengthen his authority and the interests of the crown, by effecting a reconciliation with his former rivals; and for this purpose Sir James Ormond, now the Irish leader of the Butler family, proposed an interview with the lord deputy in Dublin, to vindicate himself from some insinuations of disaffection to the present government.

This proposal being agreed to by Kildare, St. Patrick's cathedral was appointed as the place of conference, whither Sir James Ormond repaired, attended by a formidable train of armed followers. The citizens with an equal force guarded the lord deputy; but while the chiefs were engaged in adjusting their disputes a quarrel occurred amongst their attendants, and the Dublinians let fly a volley of arrows against their opponents, some of which stuck in the images in the rood-loft without doing further mischief; a profanation, in atonement for which, the mayor of Dublin was ordered by the pope to walk barefoot through the city in open procession before the sacrament on Corpus Christi day annually, a custom which was observed until the time of the Reformation. The principal parties, notwithstanding this accident, separated with formal declarations of respect and friendship, but with increased animosity on both sides.

Kildare now took a more effectual method of weakening the power of the Butlers, by giving his daughter Margaret in marriage to Pierce, the presumptive heir to the earldom of Ormond, and the rival of Sir James in his pretensions to the chieftainship. The power of the latter was for some time so great, that Pierce and his family were reduced to the greatest penury and distress, till stimulated by his wife, a lady of high spirit, he issued forth from his retreat, encountered and slew his rival, and thus regained the authority and possessions to which he was entitled. The marriage of another daughter of Kildare with William Bourke of Clanrickard, led to results still more serious. Bourke ill-treated his wife, which produced such a violent effect on the irritable temper of the earl, that he remonstrated with his son-in-law in terms of great severity, and mutual defiances ensued which ended in a war between the great chieftains of Connaught and the lord deputy.

Clanrickard was joined upon this occasion by O'Brien of Thomond and others of the Munster princes; while Kildare, supported by the lords of the Pale, O'Neil, O'Donnel, and many of the other northern dynasts, took the field in all the state of a chief governor, as if he were about to engage for the honor of his sovereign, rather than to avenge a private quarrel. Clanrickard and his confederates obtained possession of Galway, with the most numerous army that had ever assembled since the arrival of the English; but, nothing daunted at their superior force, the lord deputy entered Connaught, and on the 19th of August, 1504, both armies met at the hill of Knocktuadh, about seven miles north-west of Galway.

When the lords of the Pale viewed the strength of their enemies, and recollected that they were engaged in a private quarrel, they appeared when called to a council of war generally inclined to a retreat: but Nugent lord Delvin, exclaimed, "My learning is not such that with a glorious tale I can utter my stomach; but I promise to God and the princes, I shall be the first that shall throw the first spear among the Irish in this battle. Let him speak now that will, for I have done!" He fulfilled his promise, for a little before the battle joined, he spurred his horse, threw a small spear among the enemy which killed one of the Bourkes, and then returned to the troop which he commanded. Encouraged by this boldness, the chiefs resolved to keep their ground, and the first tumultuous onset was received with such steadiness by the archers of the Pale, and repelled with such execution, that the insurgents fled on all sides, and were pursued nearly to the gates of Galway with prodigious slaughter; while on the part of the victors scarcely any loss was sustained, except that of a few prisoners that were abandoned by Gerald, the son of the lord deputy, who rashly quitted his station in the rear to partake in the engagement. Kildare was about to enter the town immediately after the victory, but O'Donnel wisely restrained him, saying "Many of our people are overpowered and slain, and others of them separated from us; I therefore think it better to remain this night on the field as a sign of our victory, and to form our camp—our scattered troops will then return to us upon seeing our standards and colours." The deputy followed this counsel; the next morning he entered Galway in triumph, took Clanrickard and his sons prisoners, and the archbishop of Dublin was sent to notify to the king the total overthrow of all his Irish enemies.

A few years before the battle of Knocktuadh an extraordinary instance of civic justice occurred in this town, which, in the eyes of its citizens, elevated their chief magistrate to a rank with the inflexible Roman. James Lynch Fitz-Stephen, an opulent merchant, was mayor of Galway in 1493. He had made several voyages to Spain, as a considerable intercourse was then kept up between that country and the western coast of Ireland. When returning from his last visit he brought with him the son of a respectable merchant named Gomez, whose hospitality he had largely experienced, and who was now received by his family with all that warmth of affection which from the earliest period has characterised the natives of Ireland,

Young Gomez soon became the intimate associate of Walter Lynch, the only son of the mayor, a youth in his twenty-first year, and who possessed qualities of mind and body which rendered him an object of general admiration; but to these was unhappily united a disposition to libertinism, which was a source of the greatest affliction to his father. The worthy magistrate, however, was now led to entertain hopes of a favourable change in his son's character, as he was engaged in paying honorable addresses to a beautiful young lady of good family and fortune. Preparatory to the nuptials, the mayor gave a splendid entertainment, at which young Lynch fancied that his intended bride viewed his Spanish friend with too much regard. The fire of jealousy was instantly lighted up in his distempered brain, and at their next interview he accused his beloved Agnes with unfaithfulness to him. Irritated at its injustice, the offended fair one disdained to deny the charge, and the lovers parted in anger.

On the following night while Walter Lynch slowly passed the residence of his Agnes, he observed young Gomez to leave the house, as he had been invited by her father to spend that evening with him. All his suspicions now received the most dreadful confirmation, and in maddened fury he rushed on his unsuspecting friend, who alarmed by a voice which the frantic rage of his pursuer prevented him from recognizing, fled towards a solitary quarter of the town near the shore. Lynch maintained the fell pursuit till his victim had nearly reached the water's edge, when he overtook him, darted a poinard into his heart, and plunged his body, bleeding, into the sea, which, during the night, threw it back again upon the shore, where it was found, and recognised on the following morning.

The wretched murderer, after contemplating for a moment the deed of horror which he had perpetrated, sought to hide himself in the recesses of an adjoining wood, where he passed the night a prey to all those conflicting feelings which the loss of that happiness he had so ardently expected, and a sense of guilt of the deepest dye could inflict. He at length found some degree of consolation in the firm resolution of surrendering himself to the law, as the only means now left to him of expiating the dreadful crime which he had committed against society. With this determination he bent his steps towards the town at the earliest dawn of the following morning; but he had scarcely reached its precincts, when he met a crowd approaching, amongst whom, with shame and terror, he observed his father on horseback, attended by several officers of justice. To this moment the venerable magistrate had no suspicion that his only son was the assassin of his friend and guest; but when young Lynch proclaimed himself the murderer, a conflict of feeling seized the wretched father beyond the power of language to describe. To him, as chief magistrate of the town, was entrusted the power of life and death. For a moment the strong affection of a parent pleaded in his breast in behalf of his wretched son; but this quickly gave place to a sense of duty in his magisterial capacity as an impartial dispenser of the laws. The latter feeling at length predominated, and though he now perceived that the cup of earthly bliss was about to be for ever snatched from his lips, he resolved to sacrifice all personal considerations to his love of justice, and ordered the guard to secure their prisoner.

The sad procession moved slowly towards the prison amidst a concourse of spectators, some of whom expressed the strongest admiration of the upright conduct of the magistrate, while others were equally loud in their lamentations for the unhappy fate of a highly accomplished youth who had long been a universal favourite. But the firmness of the mayor had to withstand a still greater shock when the mother, sisters, and intended bride of the wretched Walter, beheld him who had been their hope and pride, approach pale, bound, and surrounded with spears. Their frantic outcries affected every heart except that of the inflexible magistrate, but he had now resolved to sacrifice life with all that makes life valuable rather than swerve from the path of duty.

In a few days the trial of Walter Lynch took place, and in a provincial town of Ireland, containing at that period not more than three thousand inhabitants, a father was beheld sitting in judgment, like another Brutus, on his only son, and like him, too, condemning that son to die, as a sacrifice to public justice. Yet the trial of the firmness of this upright and inflexible magistrate did not end here. His was a virtue too refined for vulgar minds: the populace loudly demanded the prisoner's release, and were only prevented by the guards from demolishing the prison and the mayor's house which adjoined it; and their fury was increased on learning that the unhappy prisoner had now become anxious for life. To these ebullitions of popular rage were added, the intercessions of persons of the first rank and influence in Galway, and the entreaties of his dearest relatives and friends; but while Lynch evinced all the feelings of a father and a man placed in his singularly distressing circumstances, he undauntedly declared that the law should take its course.

On the night preceding the fatal day appointed for the execution of Walter Lynch, this extraordinary man entered the dungeon of his son, holding in his hand a lamp, and accompanied by a priest. He locked the gate.

after him, kept the keys fast in his hand, and then seated himself in a recess of the wall. The wretched culprit drew near, and with a faltering tongue, asked if he had any thing to hope. The mayor answered, "No, my son—your life is forfeited to the laws, and at sunrise you must die! I have prayed for your prosperity; but that is at an end—with this world you have done for ever—were any other but your wretched father your judge, I might have dropped a tear over my child's misfortune, and solicited for his life, even though stained with murder—but you must die—these are the last drops which shall quench the sparks of nature—and, if you dare hope, implore that heaven may not shut the gates of mercy on the destroyer of his fellow-creature. I am now come to join with this good man in petitioning God to give you such composure as will enable you to meet your punishment with becoming resignation." After this affecting address, he called on the clergyman to offer up their mutual prayers for God's forgiveness to his unhappy son, and that he might be fully fortified to meet the approaching catastrophe. In the ensuing supplications at a throne of mercy, the youthful culprit joined with fervour, and spoke of life and its concerns no more.

Day had scarcely broken when the signal of preparation was heard amongst the guards without. The father rose, and assisted the executioner to remove the fetters which bound his unfortunate son. Then unlocking the door he placed him between the priest and himself, leaning upon an arm of each. In this manner they ascended a flight of steps, lined with soldiers, and were passing on to gain the street, when a new trial assailed the magistrate, for which he appears not to have been unprepared. His wretched wife, whose name was Blake, failing in her personal exertions to save the life of her son, had flown in distraction to the heads of her own family, and prevailed on them, for the honour of their house, to rescue him, and save their name from ignominy. They flew to arms, and a prodigious concourse soon assembled to support them, whose outcries for mercy to the culprit must have shaken any nerves less firm than those of the mayor of

Galway.—He exhorted them to yield submission to the laws of their country; but finding all his efforts fruitless to accomplish the ends of justice at the accustomed place and by the usual hands, he by a desperate victory over paternal feeling, resolved himself to perform the sacrifice which he had vowed to pay on its altar. Still retaining a hold of his unfortunate son, he mounted with him by a winding stairs within the building, that led to an arched window overlooking the street, which he saw filled by the populace. Here he secured the end of the rope, which had been previously fixed round the neck of his son, to an iron staple which projected from the wall, and after taking from him a last embrace, he launched him into eternity.

The intrepid magistrate expected instant death from the fury of the populace; but the people seemed so much overawed or confounded by the magnanimous act, that they retired slowly and peaceably to their several dwellings. The innocent cause of this sad tragedy is said to have died soon after of grief, and the unhappy father of Walter Lynch to have secluded himself during the remainder of his life from all society, except that of his mourning family. His house still exists in Lombard-street, Galway, which is yet known by the name of 'Dead-man's-lane,' and under the front window are to be seen a skull and cross-bones executed in black marble.

From the battle of Knocktuadh to the death of Henry VII. which occurred in 1509, comparative tranquillity appears to have prevailed in Ireland. If you have closely studied the events of his reign, you must have observed that every effort made in this country to subvert the throne of Henry, tended only to rivet the authority of England more firmly over the island. Since the invasion of Edward Bruce in the fourteenth century, the power of the natives had been greatly strengthened; and if, during the sanguinary contests between the Yorkists and Lancastrians, they had possessed such leaders as Robert Bruce or William Wallace, the independence of Ireland would probably have been completely restored. That such an event did not take place at a period apparently so propitious, we can only attribute to the over-ruling hand of Providence, who has, no doubt, for the wisest ends, permitted a union to subsist between the two islands, for many centuries, fitful, feverish, and disturbed indeed; but which, let us hope, will end at length in one of consolidated affection, equally beneficial to the interests of both countries. However unamiable the character of Henry VII. appears, it must be acknowledged that he evinced great wisdom and moderation in his conduct towards Ireland; and we cannot but admire his prudence in overlooking the offences of the earl of Kildare, reconciling him to his interests, and entrusting him with the government of a country where his energetic valour and munificence made him at once an object of terror and affection. This active viceroy used his power with so much vigour and fidelity, that during the last ten years of this reign the crown nearly regained that authority which had been almost lost by the misrule of two centuries. The Pale was tranquillized and secured; some of the most turbulent native chieftains became the avowed friends of the English government, and a more kindly intercourse was commenced between the inhabitants of both races.

CHAPTER IV.

Accession of Henry VIII.—Death of the Earl of Kildare—Vigorous conduct of Gerald, his Son, and Successor in the Government—New Feuds between the Geraldines and Butlers— Margaret, the great Countess of Ormond— Kildare accused—His interview with Cardinal Wolsey—Anecdote of Kildare—The Earl of Surrey Lord Deputy—Insurrection of Con O'Neil—Submission of O'Neil and O'Donnel—O'More's Insurrection—Surrey's Popularity and Recall—The Irish in France —Exploit of Nicholas Walsh — Pierce (Rufus) Earl of Ormond, Lord Deputy— Murder of Talbot of Belgard—Dissensions between Ormond and Kildare—Kildare, Lord Deputy—Treasonable practices of Desmond —Kildare suspected and summoned to London—Pierce Earl of Ossory restored to power—Murder of the Bishop of Leighlin— Machinations of the Emperor Charles V.— Sir William Skeffington Lord Deputy—

Kildare restored—His ambitious and violent conduct—Secret proceedings of the Council—Kildare summoned to London — The Government is committed to Lord Thomas Fitzgerald—Rumours of Kildare's Execution—Insurrection of Lord Thomas Fitzgerald—Action at Salcock-wood—Murder of Archbishop Alan—Correspondence between Fitzgerald and Lord James Butler—Siege of the Castle of Dublin—Repulse of Fitzgerald—Arrival of Sir William Skeffington—Siege of Maynooth—Final suppression of the Insurrection—Death of the Earl of Kildare—Lord Leonard Grey, Lord Deputy—Execution of Lord Thomas Fitzgerald and his five Uncles—Escape and adventures of young Gerald Fitzgerald.

FEW princes have ascended a throne with more brilliant prospects than king Henry VIII. In the prime of youth, with an indisputable title, and a treasury become rich beyond example through the grasping and parsimonious character of his father, he assumed the sceptre of a powerful kingdom. The beauty of his person, his frank and generous manners, and his profuse grandeur soon gained him the caressess of his subjects, and the flattery of foreigners; but a love for military glory engaged him in expeditions, which, though attended by little advantage to his subjects, were conducted with a vain parade of splendor that speedily dissipated those treasures, which, if wisely employed, might have conferred solid blessings on his subjects.

Though the state of Ireland, at such a period, was necessarily neglected, Henry on his accession, had the prudence to continue the earl of Kildare in the government, and that nobleman did not relax for a moment in his efforts for maintaining the authority of the crown. Political affairs were managed with considerable prudence, while the viceroy flew in person to every part of the country where insurrection dared to raise its head. But in one of these expeditions which he undertook against the O'Mores, a powerful sept in Leix, (the Queen's county) he received a wound of which he died in October, 1513; an event that excited the greatest consternation amongst the friends of

English authority, and a proportionable degree of exultation amongst its enemies.

The great earl of Kildare, as he is justly called, left issue eight sons and six daughters, of whom Gerald, the eldest son, was appointed to succeed him in the Irish government. His name served to rally the scattered troops, and check the outrages of the disaffected; while his vigorous conduct soon evinced that he inherited his father's spirit. Having first defeated O'More, he entered Ulster, subdued the clan O'Reilly, and took the castle of Cavan. In the east he overthrew the sept of O'Toole in Wicklow; and having slain their leader, sent his head as a present to the mayor of Dublin.— He also suppressed some commotions in Munster by compelling the town of Clonmel to surrender; and by these vigorous proceedings he quickly extinguished every appearance of insubordination in the different provinces.

The period of tranquillity that ensued was short, as those feuds which had so long raged between the great families of the Geraldines and Butlers, burst forth with extraordinary violence on the death of Thomas earl of

Ormond, who was one of the most wealthy and most highly favored noblemen of the English court. Pierce Rufus (or the Red,) his successor, had married, as I have already stated, a daughter of the late earl of Kildare, an alliance which her father hoped would be the means of terminating the terrible dissensions that prevailed between those two noble houses. But the event proved quite contrary to his expectations, for this lady appears to have sacrificed all her predilections for the honor of her own family to the ambition of raising that of her husband from the state of inferiority into which it had for some time fallen in Ireland ; and the *great* countess of Ormond, as she is generally designated, appears to have possessed a character in every way fitted for such a task. An ancient writer informs us that Pierce, earl of Ormond was " himself a plain simple gentleman, saving in feats of arms ;" but that his countess was " a lady of such port, that all estates of the realm crouched unto her, and so politic, that nothing was thought substantially debated without her advice. She was manlike and of tall stature, very liberal and bountiful—a sure friend—a bitter enemy; hardly disliking where she fancied; not easily fancying where she disliked." She is said by tradition to have frequently taken unfair means to aggrandize her family at the expense of her neighbours—it appears certain, however, that she greatly improved the counties of Kilkenny and Tipperary by introducing artificers of various kinds from Flanders, who gave to the inhabitants a useful example of industry.

As the present greatness of the Kildare family proportionably depressed that of Ormond, the ambitious countess stimulated her husband to use every means in his power to supplant the lord deputy in the royal favour. Cardinal Wolsey who was at this time in the zenith of his authority, readily listened to the insinuations of Ormond, that Kildare had alienated the king's revenue, and raised his consequence by maintaining a traitorous correspondence with O'Neil and his other Irish connexions. To answer these serious charges the viceroy was summoned into England in 1519, being permitted by the king to entrust the reins of government to his kinsman, Sir Thomas Fitzgerald of Lackagh.

Soon after his arrival in London, cardinal Wolsey brought a formal accusation against the earl; and amongst other crimes, charged him with desiring to reign in Ireland as if it were his own kingdom. To which Kildare replied, with a spirit not unworthy of his father, "I would, my lord, that you and I had changed kingdoms, but for one month. I would trust to gather up more crumbs in that space, than twice the revenues of my poor earldom. But you are well and warm: so hold you, and upbraid me not with such an odious term. I slumber in a hard cabin, when you sleep in a soft bed of down. I serve under the cope of heaven, when you are served under a canopy. I drink water out of my skull, (a mean culinary vessel) when you drink wine out of golden cups. My courser is trained to the field, when your jenet is taught to amble. When you are graced, and belorded, and crouched and kneeled unto, then I find small grace with our Irish borderers, except I cut them off by the knees." At these words the council smiled, and the haughty cardinal perceiving that he had no simpleton to deal with, rose from the table in a fume, and deferred the trial of the business until further proofs should arrive from Ireland.

The character of Kildare was open and generous; and though irritable he was easily appeased, as appears from the following incident. While enraged at one time with some of his servants for a fault which they had committed, one of his horsemen sportively offered Boyce, his gentleman, an Irish hobby, if he would pluck a hair from the earl's beard. Boyce went up to his master respectfully, in the very tempest of his passion, and said, "If it like your lordship, one of your horsemen has promised me a choice horse, if I pluck one hair from your beard." "I agree," said the earl, "but if thou pluck any more than one, I promise thee to pluck my fist from thine ear."

As nothing except vague suspicions could be adduced against Kildare, the cardinal found it impossible to procure his condemnation, but he had sufficient influence to prevent a definitive sentence being pronounced in his favour; and he soon after found means to convince the king of the propriety of committing the government of Ireland to some English nobleman of rank and talent, who should be wholly indifferent to the various factions which distracted the country. Thomas Howard, earl of Surrey, son to that duke of Norfolk who had conquered the Scots at Flodden, was accordingly appointed to the high office; while means were found to appease the injured feelings of Kildare, whose consequence had been increased since his arrival in England by his marriage with lady Elizabeth Grey, daughter of the marquis of Dorset. He was pronounced clear of every imputation on his honour; and in the following year he accompanied the king into France with a magnificent retinue, and was present at the celebrated interview of Henry and Francis I. between Ardres and Guisnes.

Surrey, in the mean time, had commenced the administration of the Irish government with a vigour and prudence which promised the greatest success. The Ulster chieftain, Con O'Neil, nicknamed *Baccagh* or the Limper, having made a furious inroad into Meath, the viceroy marched against him with such celerity that the invader retired precipitately to his fastnesses, and, alarmed at the activity displayed by the new viceroy, he speedily sent an embassy to Dublin, desiring to be received into the favour and protection of the government, and promising that his future conduct should prove the sincerity of his attachment to the crown. Surrey received the embassy in the most favourable manner, and transmitted an account of O'Neil's submission to the court of England, adding, that he considered it a presage of the general tranquillization of the island, which could be best effected by admitting the whole nation to the benefits of English law. O'Donnel, another northern chieftain, who had lately returned from Rome, made about the same time the warmest professions of attachment to the viceroy; and to encourage these loyal demonstrations, Surrey was empowered to confer on them the honour of knighthood: a collar of gold was also presented to O'Neil in the name of the king, with an invitation to visit the court of England. Still the means were neglected of breaking the power of those turbulent chieftains by imparting to the entire population those privileges of English law and protection which they had so frequently sought since the reign of Edward III.

O'Neil's invasion had scarcely been repelled when the viceroy was again called to the field, to suppress a furious insurrection of O'More, the chieftain of Leix, an expedition in which the valour and conduct of lord Surrey was severely tried. I would not have noticed this petty broil, but to mention the daring heroism of an Irish soldier, and the narrow escape of the lord lieutenant. In one of the many skirmishes that took place, the earl pursued the flying enemy at the head of his cavalry. One of O'More's followers, reckless of his life, resolved, if possible, to check the advance of the royal forces by killing their noble leader; and concealing himself for this purpose at the side of a wood, he discharged his piece full in the viceroy's face. The ball struck the visor of his helmet, which was providentially down, and penetrated no further, while the Irishman was pursued by some English soldiers who cut him in pieces. O'More for the present, escaped to his strong holds, but Surrey adopted such measures to cut off his resources, as soon reduced him to submission.

Lord Surrey spent two years in his government of Ireland, and though nearly the whole of that period was occupied by him in military service, he showed a sincere anxiety to promote the best interests of the country. His impartial justice, wise moderation, and magnificent hospitality, gained for him the affections of a highly susceptible people, while he watched over the interests of the crown with a vigilant circumspection. He laid before the court of England some plans for reforming the state of the country committed to his care, which might have been productive of the happiest effects; but, unfortunately, they were as usual disregarded, and the island was still left a prey to anarchy and confusion. In the eyes of the vain-glorious Henry, a foreign war, from which he could derive no solid advantage, was considered of more importance than the tranquillization of so fair a portion of his dominions; and the earl of Surrey was removed from a government which he had so wisely administered, to lead the armies of his sovereign into France.—His departure was witnessed with deep regret by the people of both races; and when the king's pleasure was signified to raise a body of troops among the native Irish, they flocked in crowds to the standard of their late revered viceroy. Seven hundred of those volunteers, under the command of lord Le Poer, were mustered in St. James's Park, London, to the no small amazement of the English; and their fierce bravery and too often irregular mode of warfare, seemed to justify the epithet of 'wild Irish,' by which they had been so long distinguished in the sister island. When sometimes acting as purveyors to the army, they are said to have practised the following method of obtaining a supply of provisions. Having caught a bull, they tied him to a stake and scorched him with burning faggots till the cries of the tortured animal attracting the cattle in every direction, they were easily conveyed to the camp. Such of the Irish as were made prisoners by the enemy were put to death in the most cruel manner, and the Irish did not fail to retaliate on all Frenchmen who fell into their hands. Of their personal valour in this war, many anecdotes are told, one of which I shall relate. At the close of the siege of Boulogne, a body of French troops encamped on the west side of the town, beyond the haven, and one of them had the hardihood to challenge any man of the English army to come over and meet him in single combat. Though every circumstance was in favour of the challenger, the place of combat being at his own side of the haven, and the passage over very wide, yet Nicholas Walsh, an Irish soldier, accepted the challenge, swam across the water, slew his antagonist, and returned to his own party with the Frenchman's head in his mouth. Accounts like these may give some idea of the intrepidity and semi-barbarism of the native Irish of that period. Nor was this latter quality confined to the Irish soldiers; unhappily, the military annals of all nations abound with instances of ferocity not less revolting to humanity than those which I have narrated.

The earl of Surrey, during his administration of the Irish government, had given his fullest confidence to the rivals of Kildare, and at his instance, Pierce earl of Ormond, was appointed his successor. The native chieftains, who had so lately submitted, now took advantage of the great reduction of the military force, to renew their private quarrels; and civil strife so raged in various quarters of the country, that the chief governor was frequently called upon to arbitrate between the contending factions, the leaders of whom made peace and war with all the independence of sovereign princes. A singular incident of this kind occurred in 1522.—Mac Gillaphadruig, or Fitzpatrick, the Irish chieftain of Ossory, conceiving himself to have been aggrieved by the lord deputy, resolved to seek redress from king Henry, not as a subject, but as a sovereign. He accordingly sent an ambassador to the English court, who meeting the king at the door of his private chapel, delivered his commission in the following words with the most solemn gravity: *Sta pedibus, Domine Rex! Dominus meus Gillapatricius me misit ad te, et jussit dicere, quod si non vis castigare Petrum Rufum, ipse facit bellum contra te.* (Stand, my lord, O king!—My lord Gillpatrick has sent me to thee, and commanded me to say, that if you do not chastise Peter the Red, he will make war upon thee.) Henry treated the ambassador with silent contempt; Peter the Red was not chastised; and the power of Fitzpatrick did not enable him to resent the affront.

The difficulties of Ormond's government were increased at this time by the return of Kildare to Ireland, who soon commenced secret practices against his old rival, which a sanguinary incident that occurred in the winter of 1522 fanned into an open flame. While Talbot of Bellgard, a trusty friend of the earl of Ormond, was on his way to Dublin to keep his Christmas with the lord deputy, he was assassinated near Ballymore by James Fitzgerald, one of the Kildare family. The murderer was seized, sent to London, and by the orders of Wolsey, led through the streets of that metropolis, haltered and manacled preparatory to his execution; but the duke of Suffolk, father-in-law to Kildare, had at this time great influence at the English court, and Fitzgerald was ultimately pardoned. Meantime mutual accusations being preferred by Kildare and Ormond, commissioners were sent to Ireland to inquire into the allegations of each party; but in the examination which followed, Kildare received such support from his powerful connexions in England, that sentence was again pronounced in his favour; and to complete his triumph he was appointed to supersede his antagonist in the Irish government.

The ambitious rivalry of these two great families did not terminate here: all the actions of the new deputy were watched with a jealous eye by his disappointed adversaries; and events soon occurred which enabled them once more to fill the English court with suspicions of Kildare's designs. His kinsman, James earl of Desmond, who had lately succeeded his father Maurice, manifested all the restlessness of his most ambitious ancestors, and carried his opposition to the English government to such a length, that in the year 1524, he engaged in a league offensive and defensive with Francis I. of France, against the king of England. Henry was so enraged when he heard of this transaction, that he issued orders to the lord deputy to use the most vigorous efforts to seize the person of the earl of Desmond. Kildare made a show of obedience, but after penetrating a little way into Munster, some insurrectionary movements in the north afforded him a sufficient pretext for giving up the pursuit of his kinsman. This conduct was urged at the court of London as a proof that he had formed traiterous connexions with the king's enemies, and secretly supported the earl of Desmond in his treasonable proceedings. To answer these serious charges he was again ordered to England, and committed to close confinement, from whence he was at length released by the interposition of his English friends, a large number of whom became sureties for his future obedience.

Lord Delvin, who succeeded Kildare in the Irish government, was quickly engaged in hostilities with the native chieftains, and at a parley with O'Connor of Offaley, was treacherously seized and made prisoner. This paved the way for the restoration to power, in 1528, of Pierce, earl of Ossory, (he having about this time resigned the title of Ormond, at the king's request, to Sir Thomas Bullen,) but neither his own vigour, nor the masculine understanding of his countess, was sufficient for the government of a country a prey to factions excited or supported by his still powerful rivals, and filled with disorders of various kinds. Doran, bishop of Leighlin, an excellent prelate, had been lately murdered by Maurice Kavanagh, his own archdeacon, whom he had reproved for some misconduct. Lady Slane, a daughter of Kildare, found means to involve the deputy with the numerous partisans of the Irish race; while the emperor Charles V. in revenge for the process which Henry had commenced to procure a divorce from Catherine of Arragon, was endeavouring to raise an insurrection in Ireland, and for this purpose, in imitation of his rival Francis I. had entered into a negociation with the earl of Desmond. But this treaty proved as unavailing as the former, for this vain-glorious chief received soon after a signal overthrow from his uncle at Mourne-abbey near Mallow, and died in the following year.

Henry now hoped in some measure to remedy the disordered state of Ireland by sending over an English chief-governor. He accordingly appointed Sir William Skeffington to that office, with Kildare, again restored to favour, as his chief-adviser, who vigorously co-operated in the viceroy's efforts to maintain tranquillity, till, delivered by the fall of cardinal Wolsey from the apprehensions he entertained of his power, he determined no longer to act a subordinate part; and finding means to have Skeffington recalled in 1532, the reins of government were entrusted once more to his own hands. Having now apparently vanquished all his enemies, he is said to have indulged the most ambitious designs of exalting his family and partisans, and depressing the power of his rivals. Assuming all the rude state of an Irish prince, the native chieftains flocked around him, and were received as his kinsmen and associates. Contrary to an existing law he gave one of his daughters in marriage to O'Connor of Offaley, and another to the prince of Ely O'Carrol. Having become involved in the private feuds of the former, he received a shot in the head at the siege of Birr, which is said to have disordered his intellects, and added to the subsequent confusion of his administration. Continually surrounded by an armed rabble, he could at all times support his partisans, and execute vengeance on his enemies, amongst whom the earl of Ossory and his family were treated with particular rigour, and their lands ravaged and invaded without mercy.

While the deputy was thus thoughtlessly gratifying his ambition or vengeance, the majority of the council were forming plans for his complete overthrow, under the guidance of Ossory, Allan, archbishop of Dublin, and some other individuals of influence and sagacity. After various secret meetings, they in 1534 agreed to present a memorial to the king, which detailed all the grievances of the subject, and the disorders of the state. It asserted that the extent of English laws, manners, language, and habit was now reduced to the narrow compass of twenty miles. This evil is attributed to the illegal exactions and oppressions which had driven the English tenantry from their settlements; the tribute they were compelled to pay to the Irish lords for a precarious protection; the rabble of disaffected Irish that were placed on their lands, and the alienation of the crown lands, which by reducing the revenue to a state of dangerous insufficiency, left the realm without succour or resource. Many of the public disorders were ascribed by the memorial to a too frequent change of chief-governors; and it besought the king's highness in future to intrust the charge of his Irish government to some loyal subject sent from his realm of England, and whose sole object should be to support the honor and interests of the crown, unconnected with Irish factions.

Henry, with his usual violence and precipitation, fixed on the earl of Kildare as the chief cause of all these evils, and commanded him immediately to repair to London, committing the government to some person for whom he would be responsible. The viceroy was forced to obey; and his last acts consummated the folly and imprudence of his government. He delivered the sword of state to his son Thomas, a youth, vain, rash, and obstinate, who had not yet attained his twenty-first year; and as he had good reason to fear that the outrages which he had committed on his rivals would be severely retaliated during his absence, he provided his castles with arms and ammunition from the public stores, contrary to the king's peremptory prohibition.

It soon appeared evident that lord Thomas Fitzgerald was deficient in the qualifications most necessary for the government of the country at such a crisis. His person and external endowments were indeed well calculated to excite public admiration ; but to the rashness of youth he added a great portion of family pride, an unbounded confidence in the power of the Geraldines, and an insolent contempt for the rivals of his house. The lords of the council soon became offended at his petulance, and he was in no less danger from the suspicious vigilance of his enemies than the adulation of his friends. Intelligence having arrived that his father had been committed to the Tower, each party watched the movements of the other with the greatest jealousy, and the capital was filled with rumours and conjectures. A correspondence was kept up between the enemies of the Geraldines in England and

Ireland, and one of the letters transmitted on this occasion was said to have been brought away accidentally from the apartment of a priest by John de la Hide, a friend of lord Thomas, which announced the execution of the earl in the Tower, and the meditated destruction of his whole family. The young deputy gave too ready an ear to the fatal intelligence, and being instigated by his Irish kinsmen O'Neil and O'Connor, he determined to renounce his allegiance to the supposed destroyer of his father, and plunged at once into a rash and desperate rebellion.

There was a mixture of magnanimity and folly in his first proceedings. On the 11th of June, 1534, he assembled at the castle of Kilmainham, then the residence of the chief-governor, about one hundred and forty Irish horsemen, at whose head he rode through the capital in his robes of state, accompanied by his uncles, Sir John and Oliver Fitzgerald, James and John de la Hide, Burnet of Ballgriffen, Bath of Dollardstown, Field of Buske, and Rorke, a famous pirate. They rushed tumultuously to the council, who were at this time assembled in St. Mary's abbey, and who, when lord Thomas entered their chamber, rose respectfully, expecting that he would take his place. But this the young deputy declined, and requesting them to be seated, thus addressed them:—

"Howsoever injuriously we be treated, and forced to defend ourselves in arms, yet say not hereafter, but that in the open hostility which we here proclaim, we have showed ourselves no villains or churls, but warriors and gentlemen. This sword of estate is yours, not mine; I received it with an oath, and have used it to your benefit: I should offend mine honour if I turned the same to your annoyance, now that I have need of mine own sword, which I dare trust. As for this sword it flattereth me with a golden scabbard; but it hath in it a pestilent edge, already bathed in the Geraldines' blood, and whetted for further destruction. Save yourselves from us as from your open enemies. I am no longer Henry's deputy, I am his foe. I am more disposed to meet him in the field, than to serve him in office; I have more mind to conquer than to govern ; and if all the hearts of England and Ireland that have cause thereto, would join in this quarrel, as I trust they will, then should he be a by-word, as I hope he shall, for his heresy, lechery, and tyranny, wherein the age to come may score him among the ancient princes of most abominable and hateful memory."

When the young deputy had terminated his violent harangue, Cromer, the primate, took him calmly by the hand, and pathetically remonstrated with him on the rashness and wickedness of an attempt at rebellion, grounded on uncertain rumour, and totally unjustifiable, even if that rumour were confirmed. He warned him against the folly of believing that he could subdue the kingdom by force, or retain it against the power of king Henry; and he predicted, that if he persevered in the purpose which he had just avowed, he would involve his country in desolation and carnage, his whole family in ruin and dishonour, and himself in the terrible guilt of shedding innocent blood. "Yea," added the good primate, "the child is not yet born that shall feel the smart of this day's uproar."

While Cromer was delivering his speech, which he did with much emotion, some of the followers of Lord Thomas, who did not understand a word of English, fancied that the primate was encouraging their young chief in his enterprise, and one of the Irish bards, who always attended on such occasions, instantly burst into a strain of impassioned verse in praise of the hero, whom he designated as the gallant *silken lord*, a title by which he was generally distinguished, on account of the richness of his dress, and the splendour of his train. The rhapsodist chided his delay and called him to the field, and the young Geraldine unhappily was more influenced by the romantic effusion of the bard, than by the sage councils of the prelate of Armagh. Throwing down the sword of state, he rushed precipitately from the council; and as Dublin had been lately much weakened by the plague, he was permitted for some days to hover about the city, collecting his forces, and arranging his plan of operations.

He was speedily joined by the O'Tooles of Wicklow, and some other Irish septs, with whom traversing the English pale, he compelled the inhabitants to take an oath of fidelity to his cause, on pain of imprisonment : and he sent emissaries to the pope, and the emperor Charles V. intreating their assistance. As the devastation of Fingal, the principal granary of Dublin, now menaced the citizens with famine, they sent some forces for its protection ; but these were defeated near Salcock-wood, and eighty of them slain. Emboldened by this success, lord Thomas approached the gates of Dublin, and threatened to deliver up the city to destruction, unless he were permitted to lay siege to the castle, where archbishop Allan, and some other enemies of the Geraldines had taken refuge. The constable of the castle, which was then defended by strong walls and towers, and encompassed by a broad and deep moat, relying on the security of the fortress, permitted the citizens to save their habitations from ruin, by accepting lord Thomas's terms ;* but Allan,

* The castle was well supplied by the citizens upon this occasion : alderman Fitzsimmons furnished on his own account, twenty tuns of wine, twenty-four tuns of beer, twenty thousand dried ling, and sixteen hogsheads of powdered beef.

filled with terror at the recollection that he had been the chief instrument in procuring the disgrace of Kildare, had a vessel prepared secretly, in which he embarked for England; but either through the ignorance or treachery of the pilot, who was a Fitzgerald, the ship was stranded near Clontarf. Allan took refuge in an adjacent house, where his retreat was quickly discovered by a party of rebels stationed at Artain, who dragged him from his bed in barbarous triumph, and brought him, naked as he was, before lord Thomas and his uncles, Sir John and Sir Oliver Fitzgerald. The unhappy prelate cast himself on his knees, and adjured his archenemy by the love he bore his maker, to spare the life of a Christian and a bishop. The young lord turned his horse from him with disdain, and exclaimed in Irish, *Beir naim a bodach*, " Away with the churl !" His sanguinary followers interpreted his orders, (whatever might have been their commander's intention) in the most cruel sense, and instantly hewed the archbishop to pieces.

O'Neil and some other Irish chieftains, now joined the standard of rebellion, and lord Thomas, forgetful of the deadly feuds which had so long subsisted between his family and the house of Butler, made an effort to associate lord James, the eldest son of the earl of Ossory, with him in his insane project. He entreated him by a trusty messenger, to call to mind their near affinity; he invited him to unite with their countrymen in rescuing the land from the oppression of a tyrant, and he expressly proposed that when Ireland was reduced by their joint efforts, that it should be equally divided between them. Butler, however, was too politic to be caught in the snare, and sent him the following blunt reply, which showed that he had as little expectation of his success as confidence in his promises. "Your notorious treason," said lord James, "hath distained your honor and shamed your kindred. You are so liberal in partaking stakes with me, that a man would ween you had no right to the game; and you are so importunate in craving my company, as if you would persuade me to hang with you for good fellowship. Think you that James Butler is so ungracious as to sell his truth for a piece of Ireland, were it so, as it cannot be, that the chickens you reckon were both hatched and feathered. Be sure, that in this quarrel, I had rather die thy enemy, than live thy partner; and the best way I can requite the kindness you proffer me, is to advise you, far as you have gone, to look well before you leap over."

Enraged at this reproachful rejection of his overtures, Fitzgerald entered Ossory at the head of a considerable force. Lord James Butler met him at Jerpoint near Thomastown, and slew many of his followers; but being himself severely wounded, he was obliged to retire to his house at Dunmore, and the whole princely extent of the earl's demesnes became exposed to the ravages of a barbarous enemy. In the meantime six hundred of the Geraldine forces, under captain James Field, had entered the city, and according to compact, laid siege to the castle of Dublin; but a messenger from England announcing the speedy arrival of succours, the citizens suddenly closed their gates, and thus cooping up Field and his party, cut off all communication with the surrounding country. They then briskly assailed the besiegers of the castle, some of whom plunged into the river and escaped by swimming; but the greater number were taken prisoners.

This event which Lord Thomas denominated an act of the basest treachery, diverted him from his further prosecution of the devastation of Ossory, and having collected his forces, he approached the walls of Dublin, and demanded that his men should be released. The citizens replying in terms of defiance, he immediately commenced hostilities by blocking up the castle on the south side; but the guns of the fortress having destroyed Sheep (now Ship) street, where Fitzgerald began his operations, he was compelled to move his camp to the westward. He now endeavoured to cut off the supply of water by stopping the course of the river about the town, destroyed New-street and Thomas-court, the ancient residence of his ancestors, and planted a gun against New-gate, through which he purposed to force an entrance. But the citizens became at this time much encouraged by secret intelligence that many who were compelled to follow in the train of Fitzgerald's tumultuary army were well affected to the king's interests, and this was confirmed by the fact that numbers of the arrows which had been shot into the town were headless, while some of them conveyed letters of intelligence to the besieged. They now in considerable force rushed out at the gate, which the Irish had set on fire, and exclaiming that the royal army had arrived, dispersed the assailants with the loss of a hundred of their number.

Lord Thomas with difficulty eluded the pursuit of his enemies, and took refuge in the house of the Grey Friars, in Francis-street, till the following morning, when having joined the remnant of his shattered forces, he took up another position in the neighbourhood, and opened a negociation with the citizens, by which he proposed to raise the siege, and restore a number of their children who had been removed from Dublin during the plague, provided they would release his men, use their good offices to procure his pardon and that of his confederates, and supply him with money, ammunition, and artillery. The two first propositions were agreed to by the citizens, but the last was rejected; and the young Geraldine was reduced to such extremities, that he was forced to submit.

He now proceeded to inspect the situation of his strong castle of Maynooth; a duty from which he was quickly recalled by the arrival of some English troops in the harbour of Dublin. A detachment had already made good their landing; but he attacked and completely discomfited them before they had gained the city, though he was himself encountered and wounded in single combat by the English commander. After this exploit, he planted his artillery on the hill of Howth, and cannonaded the English transports with such effect, that the greater number were compelled to put to sea; and a vessel laden with horses was captured. But notwithstanding these disasters, Sir William Brereton, a renowned English knight, found means to land on the opposite side of the harbour, with five hundred men; and being soon followed by Sir William Skeffington, the new lord deputy, with a fresh body of troops and several distinguished officers, they entered the city amidst public rejoicings and acclamations, which filled the rebels at Howth with such dismay, that they struck their camp and retired.

Skeffington having received information that lord Thomas intended to lay siege to Drogheda, marched towards that town; but finding that on the contrary he had retreated into Connaught, the deputy returned to Dublin, where a lingering illness detained him during the winter. Fitzgerald in the mean time threw strong garrisons into his castles of Maynooth, Rathangan, Portlester, Carlow, Leix, and Athy; and encouraged by O'Neil and O'Connor, he soon again found himself at the head of a large tumultuary army.

In the spring of 1535, Sir William Brereton laid siege to Maynooth, which was then accounted one of the best furnished castles in Ireland. The garrison replied to his summons in terms of defiance, and for fourteen days repelled every attack of the besiegers; nor is there a doubt that they would have held out till relieved by lord Thomas, but for the treachery of the governor. This man, whose name was Christopher Paresc, was Fitzgerald's foster-brother: yet sacred as this tie was held in those days, he agreed, for a bribe, to betray his trust. Having contrived to intoxicate the garrison, the English scaled the walls at the moment of their inebriety, and soon made themselves masters of the fortress. The traitor immediately proceeded to Dublin to receive his reward; and when he appeared before the deputy, he recounted the benefits he had received from Fitzgerald, as if the reward should be proportioned to his ingratitude. Sir William Skeffington viewed the wretch with indignation and contempt. "How," said he, "couldst thou betray the trust reposed in thee by so kind a master." Then, turning to his officers, he said, "Pay this traitor the money, then off with his head." He was paid his hire, and instantly led to execution.

Lord Thomas was on his march to the relief of Maynooth, at the head of seven thousand men, when the fatal intelligence of its surrender once more baffled his hopes, and dispersed his army. With the few that remained faithful he, with a desperate rashness, sought to encounter the lord deputy: but his hasty levies fled at the first discharge of the English artillery, and one hundred and forty who fell into the hands of the royal forces, were put to death without mercy. Deserted by his followers, the unhappy youth now became a wretched outlaw, till after many hair-breadth escapes, he contrived to get into Munster, where he probably entertained hopes of obtaining assistance from his relatives of the house of Desmond. But fierce domestic dissensions raging at this time among the members of that family, the royal influence was powerful enough to restrain them from giving any effectual countenance to the rash rebellion of their kinsman. James, the confederate of Francis I. of France, had died some years before. Thomas, his uncle and successor, enjoyed his honour but five years; and his son James, who was educated at the court of England, was murdered soon after his return to his native country, by his cousin, Sir Maurice Fitzgerald. Such was, at that period, the wretched state of society in Ireland.

Lord Leonard Grey, one of the most efficient officers under the lord deputy, pursued the young Geraldine into Munster; but the difficulties attendant on an expedition into a country of which his partisans were in a great measure ignorant, soon pointed out the necessity of resorting to stratagem rather than force for effecting the suppression of this dangerous insurrection. Proposals were accordingly made to lord Thomas of the most favorable description as respected his personal safety, which are said to have been sealed by a solemn participation of the sacrament: and O'Neil and O'Connor having just made their peace with the government, Fitzgerald consented to dismiss his troops, and attend lord Grey to Dublin; who was soon after appointed lord deputy, on the death of Sir William Skeffington.

In the mean time the unhappy author of all these disasters had proceeded to London to cast himself at the king's feet in the full confidence of pardon. But king Henry was now so prejudiced against the house of Fitzgerald, that he would attend to no mediation; and while lord Thomas was on his way to Windsor, he was arrested, and conveyed to the Tower. Here he was at length convinced of his folly, when he learned that his father had not been put to death by the king, but had sunk the victim of his own rash and outrageous rebellion. He now found himself, by the death of his father, earl of Kildare; but this dignity he was suffered to enjoy for a very short period: and so furious was the vindictive monarch against the whole lineage of Kildare, that he ordered lord Grey to seize his five uncles, three of whom opposed the late insurrection, and send them prisoners to London. To accomplish the king's wish, artifice was necessary, and the deputy, accordingly, invited to a banquet Sir James Fitzgerald of Leixlip, with his brothers Sir John, Oliver, Richard, and Walter; and after entertaining them in a style of the most cordial hospitality, he suddenly seized and sent them on board a ship bound for London. It is said, that during the voyage, they maintained their courage, till the captain accidentally informed them that his ship was named " the Cow;" when they recollected with terror an old prophecy, ' that the five sons of an earl should be carried to England in a cow's belly, but should never return.' They were all, with their unfortunate nephew, convicted soon after of high treason, and executed at Tyburn on the 3d of February, 1536.

Nor did the royal vengeance stop here, for every male branch of this unfortunate family was sought out with the most vindictive jealousy. Two sons of Gerald, earl of Kildare, by his marriage with lady Elizabeth Grey, still remained, viz. Gerald, now in his thirteenth year, and Edward, in his ninth. The latter was secreted in England by the Suffolk family till the king's fury passed over.

The romantic adventures of young Gerald Fitzgerald require more particular notice. At the time of the arrest of his brother and uncles, he was lying sick of the small-pox at Donore, in the county of Kildare, from whence he was secretly conveyed in a basket by his tutor, Thomas Leverous, afterwards bishop of Kildare, first to his sister, lady Mary O'Connor of Offaley, then to the neighbourhood of Limerick, and afterwards to Kilbritton, in the county of Cork, the seat of his aunt Eleanor, who was the widow of Mac Arthy Reagh, prince of Carbery. This lady consented to marry O'Donnel, the chief of Tyrconnel, on the express condition that he should protect her young nephew; but soon discovering that her husband had entered into a treaty with the English government for betraying his ward, she made up a hundred and forty gold Portuguese pieces, and with them completely equipped young Gerald and his tutor, and transported them into France; and as soon as their escape was secured, she upbraided O'Donnel with his perfidy, and indignantly withdrew from his society and habitation.

Young Gerald was well received by the king of France; and when the English ambassador demanded him as a rebel to his sovereign, he was permitted to escape to Flanders. Thither he was pursued by one Sherlock, an emissary of the ambassador; but the governor of Valenciennes committed Sherlock to prison, and suffered Fitzgerald to proceed to Brussels. At this capital the unhappy youth became again the object of persecution, but fortunately escaped to Liege, where the prince-bishop took him under his protection; and at the recommendation of the emperor, allowed him one hundred crowns per month for his expenses.

From hence, after some time, his kinsman, cardinal Pole, removed him to his palace at Rome, where he spent three years. He then entered the service of the Knights of Malta; on many occasions he acted in a manner which reflected honour on his high descent, and was at length appointed master of the horse to the grand duke of Tuscany. During his various peregrinations, he is said to have had many singular adventures and hair-breadth escapes. One day, while hunting in company with cardinal Farnese, his horse fell with him into a pit of vast depth. But, providentially, in his descent, he caught hold of some bushes or roots, which projected from the side of the pit, and thus the rapidity of his descent was diminished; and while his horse, tumbling precipitately to the bottom, was instantly killed, the gallant youth, struggling from bush to bush, was enabled to drop unhurt upon him. In this situation he remained for three hours, until a favourite dog, having missed his master, traced him to the pit, and, by his piteous howlings, attracted the attention of the company to his perilous situation.

Thus was young Gerald Fitzgerald mercifully preserved to restore the ancient house of Kildare to its pristine honours. After the death of his royal persecutor, he returned to England, where a highly gifted mind and elegant manners, soon made him an object of general admiration. He became a particular favourite with king Edward VI. and was ultimately restored to all the honours and possessions of his family.

CHAPTER V.

Alterations in Religion — Obstacles to the Establishment of the King's Supremacy in Ireland—Archbishop Browne—Opposition of Primate Cromer to the new changes—The Parliament declares the King Supreme Head of the Church—Suppression of Monasteries—Alarming Discontents excited by the Court of Rome—Arrest and Suicide of Thaddeus Byrne—Insurrection of O'Neil and the Northern Chieftains—Battle of Bellahoe—Fleming Lord Slane—Recall and Execution of Lord Leonard Grey—Tragical death of James Earl of Ormond—Activity of Sir William Brereton—Sir Anthony St. Leger, Lord Deputy—Henry VIII. proclaimed King of Ireland—Distinguished Reception of the Irish Chieftains at Greenwich—New Civil and Ecclesiastical Regulations—Commercial Disputes between Limerick and Galway—Piracies of Sir Finneen O'Driscol—Destruc-

tion of *Dunalong Castle by the Waterfordians—Extraordinary Escape of Lieutenant Grant—Introduction of Stage Plays into Ireland.*

HITHERTO religion had no part in the factious warfare which for nearly four centuries polluted the soil of Ireland, as the two races that struggled for superiority professed the same creed, and occasionally submitted the decision of their disputes to the Roman pontiff as the supreme arbiter of their affairs. Henceforth the sacred name of religion is to become not only a strong line of demarcation between the inhabitants of English and Irish descent, but to split the English themselves into two factions, who, some from pure conviction, and others from less worthy motives, embraced the side of the king or the pope.

The religion of Ireland is an important subject which would itself require a volume of Stories. I shall, therefore, in this work notice it no farther than what is absolutely necessary to elucidate those transactions in our history, with which it is inseparably interwoven; transactions presenting the singular anomaly of a nation clinging with pertinacity to a foreign religious yoke originally imposed on them by a people whose civil domination they detested.

Whatever may have been the peculiar system of Christianity which prevailed in Ireland under our native kings, it is very generally acknowledged, that its church was wholly independent of the Roman See, till after the conversion of the Irish Danes in the eleventh century. Gillebert, bishop of Limerick, first exercised the legatine authority in this country in the year 1110, and in 1154, pope Eugene III. conferred palls on our archbishops. In 1172, the Synod of Cashel confirmed pope Adrian's grant of the kingdom of Ireland to Henry II. and the papal yoke was completely rivetted upon the country. From this period to that of which I write, the annals of the Irish church consist almost wholly of disputes between the popes and the kings of England respecting the appointment of bishops—remonstrances of the clergy against the admission of foreigners into the church, and quarrels of great violence and long duration between the archbishops of Ar-

ALTERATIONS IN RELIGION.

magh and Dublin respecting precedence. Matters of higher importance began now to demand the attention, and exercise the talents of statesmen and theologians.

The universal power over the consciences of men which had for ages been arrogated by the Roman pontiff had, during a long period, been vigorously opposed by intrepid spirits in different countries in Europe, but comparatively with little success till the glorious discovery of the art of printing dispelled the darkness of the cloister, and burst the fetters which had so long enthralled the human mind. The Bible, from which alone the pure doctrines of Christianity could be learned, was inaccessible to all men but the clergy, till the invention of this noble art, by facilitating the multiplication of copies of the sacred writings, caused them to be more generally known and better understood. In the early part of the sixteenth century, the corrupt state of the church and the necessity of a Reformation were very generally acknowledged throughout Europe; but men differed widely with regard to the mode of effecting these important objects: for while one party asserted that the lopping off some external abuses was only necessary, the other contended that nearly the whole system of the Romish religion, both in doctrine and discipline, was opposed to the word of God, and therefore required a radical change. Before the middle of that century Reformers of this description abounded in every country of Europe; and in many parts of Germany, Switzerland, and the north of Europe, the supremacy of Rome was utterly renounced, and the reformed religion permanently established.

The political state of England was, at this time, peculiarly favourable to the plans of the Reformers. The inflexible obstinacy of the papal see in refusing its sanction to the repudiation of queen Catherine, had roused the irritable and determined temper of Henry, who, from being the avowed champion of papal authority, at once became its bitterest opponent, and resolved to abrogate the Pope's authority, and suppress all monasteries in his dominions. He meditated, however, no change in the doctrines or formularies of the Church of Rome; on the contrary, to check any attempt of this nature, he published his Six Articles, which, like a two-edged sword, menaced alike the abetters of the pope's supremacy, and the impugners of transubstantiation; and both parties too frequently felt the keenness of its edge.

As the sincere partisans of the Reformation were extremely numerous in England, and the great body of the people attached to the crown, Henry found little difficulty in obtaining his wishes in that country. He was accordingly declared, by the convocation and the parliament, to be supreme head, on earth, of the church of England, and invested with all the powers annexed to that supremacy. But in extending his new authority to Ireland, the king had obstacles to encounter of the most serious description. Here the spirit of religious inquiry had made little progress, to which bitter jealousies, perpetual civil wars, and a constant state of insecurity, were highly unfavorable. Their unquiet and uncivilized mode of life indisposed the people to any speculations of an abstruse nature, and, in all points not immediately connected with their present existence, they willingly submitted to the guidance of their clergy.

The same devoted attachment to the authority of the hierarchy, which, nearly three centuries before, had led the people of Ireland to relinquish the independence of their church, now bound them to the papal see by the strongest ties, and in this prejudice they were confirmed by an opinion which very generally prevailed, not only among the natives but the Anglo-Irish, that Ireland was a fief of the pope, in right of the church of St. Peter, by virtue of which the seignory of the kingdom had been conferred on Henry II. and that it was, therefore, profane and damnable to deny the authority of the pope in his own inheritance.

But, notwithstanding these serious obstacles, Henry resolved to establish his supremacy also over the Irish church, and Doctor George Browne, a zealous ecclesiastic, attached to the reformed party, was selected as the chief instrument for effecting this design. Having, while provincial of the Augustinian Friars, in London, become remarkable for his benevolence and the liberality of his religious sentiments, he was chosen by lord Cromwell, the king's Vicar-General, to fill the see of Dublin, become vacant by the murder of archbishop Allan; and appointed one of the commissioners for procuring an acknowledgment of the king's supremacy. But this was soon found to be an object of no easy attainment; for no sooner had the commissioners explained their instructions, than Cromer, the primate, declared against any attempt to divest the holy pontiff of his prerogative as detestable and impious; he pronounced a tremendous curse on all who should sacrilegiously acknowledge the king's supremacy; and sent messengers to the pope to represent the dangers of the church, and claim the immediate interposition of the holy father in defence of his own rights and interests in Ireland.

Archbishop Browne represented the difficulties with which he had to contend to the English government in the strongest language, and recommended that the king's supremacy over the Irish church, might be enforced, as in England, by act of parliament. Pursuant to this advice, lord Leonard Grey assembled a parliament on the 1st of May, 1536, by which the king was made supreme head of the church of Ireland, and all connexion with Rome was utterly prohibited; the first-fruits of all ecclesiastical benefices were vested in the king, and by one act twelve monasteries were suppressed. Other laws were enacted by this parliament which prohibited the payment of pensions to the Irish, or fostering or marrying with them; and it was ordained that English schools should be established in every parish, and that all who could not afford to pay for the education of their children at these schools, should bring them up to trade or husbandry.

Had the population of Ireland been previously united by the abolition of national distinctions, and an equal participation of civil rights, their deliverance from a foreign spiritual jurisdiction might have been received with gratitude, as it had been by the great majority in the sister country; but no means had been adopted by the English government to gain the affections of the native Irish, who, now forgetting their private animosities, formed one common bond of union with the discontented English lords, in defence of what their clergy taught them to consider the unquestionable rights of the Roman pontiff. Lord Leonard Grey perceived the rising storm, and took active measures to repress it. He traversed the province of Leinster, and compelled the refractory or suspected chieftains to renew their engagements to the government. He then entered Munster, where James, earl of Desmond, had commenced fierce hostilities with the Butlers, and compelled that turbulent chieftain to take the oath of allegiance at his camp near Clonmel, and deliver up his natural son as a pledge of his fidelity. But in the Butlers, now become the most powerful family in Ireland, the deputy found more obstinate antagonists. The earl of Ormond and his son having refused to attend him in his military progress, lord Grey detached a body of troops to ravage their lands. Complaints were made by both parties to the throne, which were referred to the Irish council, by whom a formal reconciliation was effected: but from this period the Butlers united with the partizans of Rome to accomplish the ruin of the lord deputy.

In the mean time archbishop Browne executed with alacrity, the royal command for removing images from the churches, which he replaced by the Creed, the Lord's Prayer, and the Ten Commandments, in gilt frames, and enforcing the oath of supremacy on the clergy; but many of them preferred expulsion from their benefices to taking this obnoxious oath. The difficulties of this zealous prelate were greatly augmented by the arrival of a private commission from Rome, which enjoined his antagonist, primate Cromer, to persevere in supporting the papal authority; empowered him to absolve all persons from their oath, who had acknowledged the king's supremacy, and to declare all those accursed who held any power, either ecclesiastical or civil, superior to that of the holy church. The agents of Rome, however, did not rest satisfied with fulminating spiritual thunders, active emissaries being sent through the North to excite the Irish chiefs to take up arms. On the 24th of June, 1538, Thaddeus Byrne, a Franciscan friar, was arrested in Dublin, upon whose person was found a letter to O'Neil, signed by the bishop of Mentz in the name of the college of cardinals, in which that chieftain was excited to draw the sword against the heretical opposers of the pope's authority; and to stimulate O'Neil's exertions, this letter stated that an ancient prophecy of St. Lazerianus, archbishop of Cashel, had been lately found, which said, that the church of Rome should surely fall when the Catholic faith was once overthrown in Ireland. Lord Grey put the friar in the pillory; but being soon after commanded to send his prisoner to England, the unhappy man, in an agony of horror and distraction, put an end to his own life.

This tragical event, however, did not prevent O'Neil from embracing the high honor which the church had conferred on him, of defending the rights of the popedom. He roused the northern chieftains to arms, and appearing once more at their head, denounced vengeance against the enemies of the church. Being joined by O'Donnel, Magennis, O'Callaghan, O'Hanlon, and other chieftains, with considerable forces, he entered Meath in the month of August, 1539, and after burning Navan and Ardee, advanced to the hill of Tarah, where he mustered his army, and collected an immense booty. But he appears to have formed no settled plan of operations, and after making an ostentatious display of his numerous forces for a few days, he retreated, with his prey, towards his own territory.

During the progress of this insurrection the lord deputy had made vigorous exertions to collect an army for its suppression. The citizens of Dublin and Drogheda flocked with alacrity to his standard, and a small reinforcement of Cheshire men arrived under Sir William Brereton, who manifested such zeal for his master's service, that though he was labouring under a fractured thigh, he insisted on being raised with pullies into his ship, that he might accompany his troop. O'Neil was already on his retreat, but lord Grey pressed on him with such celerity, that he came up with his rear-guard at a place called Bellahoe, on the borders of Meath. The Irish were numerous and advantageously posted, with a river in their front, and they appeared fully resolved to defend the passage. The English, on the other hand, were determined to force it or perish in the attempt. Fleming lord Slane, having obtained the honour of leading the vanguard, ordered Halfpenny, his standard-bearer, to enter the river; but that timid officer declining the perilous adventure, he snatched the colours from him and entrusted them to Robert de Betoa, who instantly rushed through the stream with his gallant leader, and they were ably seconded by numbers of their brave associates. When arrived on the opposite bank, they made a furious attack on the enemy, which being received with equal bravery, an obstinate battle ensued, in which the Irish maintained their ground, till dispirited by the fall of Magennis, their leader, they broke and fled in dismay towards the main-body, who being seized with the panic communicated by the fugitives, fled also precipitately to their different haunts,; and thus was this formidable force entirely dispersed, and the power of the northern chieftains for the present completely broken.

Notwithstanding the signal service which lord Grey had rendered to the crown by the victory of Bellahoe, the machinations of his enemies procured his almost immediate recall.

Soon after his return to Dublin he was commanded to entrust the reins of government to Sir William Brereton, and repair to England, where he was committed to the Tower, and various charges were brought against him of oppression, bribery, and sacrilege. Amongst other points he was accused of betraying lord Thomas Fitzgerald into a submission by a promise of pardon for the purpose of destroying him; and of favouring the escape of that lord's younger brother, Gerald, who was his nephew and favourite. On these charges he was brought to trial for high treason, and sent to the scaffold. Pierce the Red, earl of Ormond, the determined opponent of this unfortunate nobleman, had died a short time before, leaving his titles and great possessions to his son James, viscount Thurles, who after rendering some signal services to the crown in Connaught and Munster, was in 1545, appointed to the command of a body of Irish forces who sailed into Scotland to assist the earl of Lenox. The expedition proving unsuccessful, the earl returned to London, where on the 17th of October, 1546, he, with nineteen of his servants, was poisoned at a supper given at Ely-house in Holborn. Thomas, his eldest son and successor, then in his fourteenth year, was brought up at the English court with king Edward VI. with whom he was a particular favourite.

The fall of lord Leonard Grey animated the Ulster chieftains to engage in a fresh insurrection; but Sir William Brereton, imitating the example of his predecessors, marched against them with a vigour and alacrity that dispersed at once their tumultuary forces. These repeated overthrows completely paralysed the efforts of the Irish, and many of the most active insurgents of both races became solicitous to make their peace with government, amongst whom were Con O'Neil, O'Brien of Thomond, and the earl of Desmond. The latter renounced the privilege which he had obtained of absenting himself from parliament, abjured the authority of the pope, and committed the care of his favourite son to the lord deputy, to be educated in the English manner.

Such was the favourable aspect of affairs, when Sir Anthony St. Leger, was entrusted with the government of Ireland, in 1541.

Soon after the arrival of the new deputy a parliament was assembled, by which it was resolved, that to give greater weight and brilliancy to the English government, the style of the sovereign should be changed from lord, to that of king of Ireland; and that it should qe high treason to impeach this title, or to oppose the royal authority. This statute was proclaimed at St. Patrick's church in Dublin, on the 23d of January, 1542, and this important proceeding was quickly followed by the submission of all the Irish chieftains, who with many Anglo-Irish lords, renounced the papal authority in the fullest manner, and took the oath of allegiance. Con O'Neil, accompanied by the bishop of Clogher, visited king Henry at Greenwich, surrendered to him his estates and Irish titles, and covenanted to adopt the English habits, manners, and language, and to assist the king like the members of the Pale, against all his enemies. Henry received the chieftain with peculiar marks of favour, regranted him his estates by patent, and in return for the Irish titles which he had renounced, he was created earl of Tyrone; and his son Matthew, baron of Dungannon.

Other chieftains were also encouraged by these marks of royal favour to repair to London, and were received with equal respect and attention. Murrough O'Brien, head of the royal house of Thomond, was created earl of Thomond, and baron of Inchiquin; and Ulick Bourke (Mac William) was elevated to the dignity of earl of Clanrickard and baron Dunkellen. Fitzpatrick was created baron of Upper Ossory, and some of the Anglo-Irish chiefs were also raised to the dignity of the peerage. All parties seemed to vie with each other in extolling the king's power and clemency, and anxious to be attached by one common bond of loyalty to the crown. "So outrageous," says Ware, "was this spirit of devotion to the sovereign in some places, that the son of lord Upper Ossory having committed a treasonable offence, he was delivered up to the hands of public justice by his own father."

The general tranquillity which now prevailed, encouraged the lord deputy to adopt some regulations in those districts where English laws and customs had for nearly two centuries fallen into disuse, which might gradually draw the people to a civilized mode of life. These regulations remedied certain abuses in ecclesiastical affairs, inflicted severe penalties on crimes, discouraged idleness, and, intended probably as a check on extravagance in dress, *permitted noblemen to put no more than twenty cubits or bandles of linen in their shirts,* and that all inferior persons should be proportionably confined in this article of magnificence. It was not yet deemed advisable to introduce any new system of jurisprudence into the newly reformed districts; but commissioners were appointed to decide controversies in the manner of the ancient Brehons, referring all obstinate cases to the deputy and council. This plan, it was expected, would draw off the people by degrees from dependence on their chieftains, and lead them to look to the crown alone for defence and protection. These hopes were not eventually realized, yet the remainder of the reign of Henry VIII. was not disturbed by any insurrectionary movements against his government, though foreign powers did not relax in their efforts to excite the chieftains to revolt.

Commercial jealousies raged to such an extent during this reign, between the principal sea-ports on the southern and western coasts of Ireland, as frequently to occasion fierce hostilities both by sea and land. A war of this nature was carried on for twelve years between the merchants of Limerick and Galway, which was attended with some bloodshed, and terminated only by the interposition of the crown. Another piratical war was carried on between Waterford and some of the ports in the neighbourhood of Cork, in which many instances of bravery were displayed which would have been creditable to regular forces. Take the following as an instance. On the 20th of February, 1537, four ships laden with Spanish wines, and consigned to the merchants of Waterford, were driven by a tempest into Cape Clear, Kinsale, and Baltimore. Sir Fineen O'Driscol, the hero of this part of the coast, had his residence at the castle of Dunalong, or the Shipcastle, on the island of Innisherkin, and his name was dreaded from the Bristol channel to the mouth of the Shannon. The prizes which he and his natural son Gilly Duff, or Black Gilbert, took by sea or land, were stored up in the Ship-castle; and here open house was kept for the gentry and pedlars, who came from all quarters to purchase bargains of wine, brandy, drapery, or other goods—the produce of their piracies. On the tempestuous night above mentioned, Gilly Duff was rowing along the shore in his launch, when the Santa Clara appeared in distress at the entrance of Baltimore harbour. He approached to offer assistance, and proposed for three tuns of wine, to bring her safely into port. The bargain was struck, and in less than an hour she was securely moored under the castle of Dunalong. The captain and crew expressed gratitude for their deliverance, and Gilly Duff increased it by inviting them to the castle, where, he said, the fire of hospitality was never out on his father's hearth. The captain and his wearied mariners gladly accepted the invitation, and enjoyed the food and festivity of Sir Fineen O'Driscol, till sunk in sleep and wine, they left their vessel to her fate. They were instantly clapped in irons, the gallies of Gilly Duff boarded the vessel, and before morning every pipe of wine which she contained was stored in the vaults of the castle, or the cellars of the adjoining Franciscan convent.

When the merchants of Waterford received intelligence of this act of piracy, they equipped a well armed vessel, which sailed on the 3d of March for Baltimore, under the command of captain Dobbyn, who coming up suddenly with the Santa Clara, boarded her on one side, while Gilly Duff with his men fled out at the other: and after firing several guns at the castle, Dobbyn brought off his prize. But this was not a sufficient satisfaction to the Waterford merchants for the insult and injury which they had sustained ; they, therefore fitted out a squadron of three ships, well appointed and victualled, and manned by four hundred men, which sailed for Baltimore, under the command of captains Woodlock and Dobbyn. Sir Fineen O'Driscol and the inmates of Dunalong castle were still carousing over the Spanish wines, when at day dawn on a fine April morning, the watch-tower bell gave notice that a hostile squadron was in sight, and in a few minutes they cast anchor before the castle. The battlements were instantly manned, and all the artillery of the fortress opened its fire on the ships: but this was answered with such effect by Woodlock's little squadron, that a breach was speedily made, and the Waterfordians, led on by lieut. Grant, rushed to the storm with a resolution that proved irresistible; forced the barbican, burst into the castle, and hoisted St. George's standard on the top of the tower. Sir Fineen O'Driscol had already made his escape to Dunboy; but Gilly Duff, perceiving that all was lost, resolved to perish in the ruins of the castle. Seizing a flaming brand, he applied it to a powder barrel, and both victors and vanquished were instantly launched into eternity. Grant alone stood uninjured in a recess of one of the tower windows, while the flames were crackling around, and burning beams and melting lead falling on every side. At that moment lieut. Butler seeing the perilous condition of his gallant comrade, seized a cross-bow, and fastening a cord to a steel bolt, shot it up to Grant, who tying it to the stone mullion of the window, slided down in a moment and found himself secure in the arms of his companions. The men of Waterford continued five days on the island, during which they captured or destroyed seventy pinnaces belonging to O'Driscol, ruined the castle and convent, and returned in triumph loaded with booty.

The reign of Henry VIII. was memorable for the introduction of stage-plays into Ireland. The members of the different guilds or corporations of Dublin were the first actors, and we are told, that during the Christmas of 1528 the earl of Kildare was invited every day to a new play performed on a stage erected in Hoggin (now College) Green—the taylors acting Adam and Eve; the shoemakers Crispin and Crispianus; the vintners the story of Bacchus; the smiths that of Vulcan; the carpenters, Joseph and Mary; and the comedy of Ceres was performed by the bakers. The priors of St. John of Jerusalem and All Hallows caused at the same time two plays to be acted, the one representing the Passion of our Saviour, and the other the various Martyrdoms of the Apostles—

so indecently were sacred and profane subjects at that time mingled together. When Henry VIII. was proclaimed king of Ireland all the lords passed through the streets in grand procession in their parliament robes, the Nine Worthies was played, and the festivities concluded with tournaments and running at the ring with spears on horseback.

CHAPTER VI.

Accession of Edward VI.—Insurrection of O'More and O'Connor—Sir Edward Bellingham, Lord Deputy—The Earl of Desmond reclaimed—Sir Anthony St. Leger, Lord Deputy—Efforts to establish the Reformation—Proclamation enjoining the New Liturgy—Opposition of Primate Dowdall—The Bible printed—Sir James Crofts, Lord Deputy—Conference of the Clergy at St. Mary's Abbey—Flight of Dowdall—Bale Bishop of Ossory—Defeat of Sir James Crofts—Death of Edward VI.—Accession of Queen Mary—Gerald Earl of Kildare—Fitzmaurice Lord Kerry—Sir Anthony St. Leger, Lord Deputy—Ejection of the Protestant Clergy—Proceedings and Sufferings of Bishop Bale—A Jubilee—The Earl of Sussex, Lord Deputy—The Roman Catholic Worship restored—The Scotch expelled from Carrickfergus—Murder of Lord Dungannon—Hostili-

ties between O'Neil and O'Donnel—Surprise and Defeat of John O'Neil—Death of O'Cahan—Story of Dean Cole.

KING HENRY VIII. terminated his eventful reign at Westminster on the 28th of January, 1547; and the guardians of Edward VI. his infant successor, soon manifested a determination to carry the alterations in the established mode of worship much farther than that arbitrary and capricious monarch had contemplated. Henry had required nothing more than the transfer from the pope to himself of the complete control over ecclesiastical dignities and possessions; but the mind of Edward, though only in his tenth year, was already well-instructed in the principles of the Reformation; and the great majory of his counsellors were actuated, some by zeal for the purity of religion, and others by political motives, to give them a permanent establishment, by effecting a radical change in the doctrines, formularies, and discipline of the church.

While these important measures were in progress in England, precautions were adopted to guard against any fresh machinations of the papal party in Ireland to impede the Reformation in that country. Sir Anthony St. Leger was continued in a government which he had, hitherto, administered with much wisdom; and Sir Edward Bellingham, a brave and skilful commander, was sent to his support with a considerable reinforcement. This force was soon called into the field to suppress a violent insurrection of O'More and O'Connor, the chieftains of Leix and Offaley, who, after their lands had been devastated, and the old inhabitants expelled, were proclaimed traitors, and reduced to the situation of desperate fugitives. They were at length induced to attend St. Leger into England, with the hope of experiencing equal clemency with the Irish insurgents during the late reign; but they were instantly committed to prison, where O'More died soon after, and their lands being declared forfeited, were conferred on those persons by whose advice they had surrendered.

Bellingham was now rewarded with the viceroyship, which he exercised, amidst the din of factions, with a wise and moderate vigour.

which procured for him the title of *the good* Bellingham. In the year 1548 some attempts were made by Henry II. king of France, to engage the northern Irish in an insurrection against the English government; and at a meeting held by O'Neil of Tyrone, with Monluc, the French ambassador, at which Wauchop, the Roman Catholic archbishop of Armagh, was present, it was agreed to accept that king's overtures, provided his majesty supplied them with money and two thousand troops. About the same time lord Baltinglass attempted to excite an insurrection in the Pale, which was suppressed by the vigilant wisdom of the viceroy, and the offenders were reconciled to the government. Bellingham adopted the same course of liberal policy, by which he appeared anxious to prevent rather than punish rebellion, towards James, earl of Desmond, who, living on his lands in the rude independence of his ancestors, refused to obey the summons of the deputy to reside in the capital under his own inspection. The viceroy unexpectedly pierced into Munster, surprised the earl in his own house, and, by kind expostulations, prevailed on him to accompany him to Dublin, where he resided for a considerable time; and his mind became so impressed by the example and instruction of Sir Edward Bellingham, with the advantages of civilized life, that he ever after continued a loyal subject and good citizen, and expressed his gratitude, in daily prayers, for his benefactor, by the name of *the good* Bellingham. Indeed the whole object of his administration appears to have been not only to guard the interests of the crown, but to protect the people from the oppression of their tyrannical lords.

Yet this excellent chief-governor could not long resist the secret machinations of those great subjects who were dissatisfied with his administration, because it curbed their licentiousness. He was recalled, at the close of 1549, to give place to Sir Francis Bryan, one of his bitterest opponents; who, having married the widow of the late earl of Ormond, possessed, during the minority of her son, all the consequence of that great family. The new viceroy, however, was cut off by the hand of death in less than a month, and his successor,

Brabazon, quickly yielded the sword of state to Sir Anthony St. Leger, whose experience was again considered necessary to further the views of the government on the subject of religion. St. Leger was instructed to convene a parliament soon after his arrival; but he found the general disposition of the people of Ireland wholly unfavourable to the attempt, being either opposed to any change in religion as arbitrary and impious, or terrified at the papal denunciations against heresy and innovation. The expressions of these feelings had been considerably restrained during the rigorous government of Henry VIII. but in a minor reign, and when still greater compliances were required of them, they gave loud utterance to their abhorrence of what they were taught to consider an impious innovation. It must, indeed, be acknowledged, that those to whom was entrusted the extension of the Reformation in Ireland appeared to have no higher object in view than to level the outworks of the old system of religion, while they took no proper means to instruct the people in the principles of that purer faith which was recommended to their adoption. Images and relics were destroyed; abbeys and nunneries were suppressed; and the authority of Rome was abolished as far as acts of parliament could do it; but no pious zealous ministers, acquainted with the Irish language, were sent to instruct a people, the great majority of whom were ignorant of any other. "Hard is it," said Sir Thomas Cusack, the chancellor, "that men should know their duties to God and to their king, when they shall not hear teaching or preaching throughout the year—preaching we have none, which is our lack, without which the ignorant can have no knowledge." At the same time, the Romish clergy, who spoke the language of the people, were listened to with attention and affection; and in the more remote parts of the island the bishops appointed by the pope continued to enjoy their sees in defiance of the royal authority; so that wherever a bishop appointed by the king was fixed, he was sure to meet a rival of papal nomination.

Sir Anthony St. Leger, to whom the settlement of this delicate affair was entrusted, was suspected of not being over anxious for its success; a suspicion which was fully confirmed at a subsequent period. As it was not deemed prudent, in the present state of public feeling, to convene a parliament, a royal proclamation, dated the 6th of February, 1550, was addressed to the clergy, enjoining them to accept the new liturgy, which was declared to be nothing more than the prayers of the church translated into the English tongue for the edification of the people. The lord deputy having submitted it to an assembly of the prelates and clergy, Dowdall, the primate, at the head of the northern ecclesiastics, declared himself its determined opposer; exclaiming, in a tone of scorn, that every illiterate fellow might now be enabled to read mass. The deputy replied that there were, indeed, too many illiterate priests as ignorant of the language in which divine service had hitherto been performed, as the people who attended them; but the present alteration was designed to remedy this evil. Dowdall sternly warned the lord deputy to beware of the clergy's curse, and then haughtily quitted the assembly, followed by the majority of the prelates. But Browne, archbishop of Dublin, with Staples of Meath, Coyn of Limerick, Travers of Leighlin, and Lancaster of Kildare, declared their concurrence with the king's proclamation; and on the following Easter-day the new liturgy was read, for the first time, in the cathedral of Christ Church, in the presence of the lord deputy and magistrates. It was printed soon after by Humphry Powell, and this was the first book printed in Ireland. The printing of the Holy Scriptures in English quickly followed; and such was the avidity of the people to read them, that it is said one John Dele, a bookseller in Dublin, sold seven thousand copies in two years. Large Bibles were, at this time, chained to the pillars in the two cathedrals, whither the poorer classes flocked daily in crowds to read them. Had the Protestant clergy of that day been actuated by a desire for promoting Scriptural knowledge among the people, those obstacles would have easily been overcome, which afterwards produced insuperable barriers to the progress of the Reformation.

Sir Anthony St. Leger being again recalled,

his place was supplied by Sir James Crofts, a zealous Protestant, under whose administration great exertions were made to remove every vestige of the late mode of worship; but the instruction of the people continued as much neglected as ever. The soldiery in some places committed such excesses in the plunder of churches, as to call at length for the interposition of the government; and those proceedings, in connexion with the firmness exhibited by primate Dowdall, only tended to augment the affection of the people for the religion of Rome. The prelate of Armagh now resided in the abbey of St. Mary, near Dublin, taking no part in the councils of the nation, and refusing all intercourse with his conforming brethren. Sir James Crofts, soon after his arrival, addressed a letter to the indignant prelate, in which he reminded him of the obedience that he owed to his sovereign, of which Christ had left him an example. The viceroy offered to become the mediator between him and his brethren, and requested him to appoint a place for holding a conference, for the purpose of restoring order and discipline to the church of Ireland, and thus preventing the necessity of severe measures, which otherwise the sovereign might find it necessary to adopt.

Dowdall, in his reply to this letter, informed the lord deputy, that he had little hope of an amicable adjustment of the present controversy, from any conference with a number of obstinate churchmen, whose judgments and consciences were totally opposite. He, however, accepted the viceroy's offer; but maintaining the stately deportment which he had hitherto assumed, he refused to go to his lordship's palace, alleging, that it would be inconsistent with that plan of retirement which he had for some time adopted. Anxious for a settlement of the dispute, Sir James Crofts overlooked this mark of disrespect, and the whole body of the clergy waited on the primate in the great hall of Mary's-abbey, where, in the month of June, 1551, a theological dispute was held, in which Dowdall defended the Romish mass, and Staples, bishop of Meath, the Reformed mode of worship. But the discussion terminated as such public disputes generally end. Each party claimed the victory, and retired from the contest still more embittered against the other.

As the Reformation had not yet been established in Ireland by a parliamentary enactment, the refractory prelate could not be legally punished; but the government found means to wound his feelings in the most tender point, by rendering his see subordinate to that of Dublin. A contest for precedence had subsisted for ages between the archbishops of Armagh and Dublin, which had been terminated at length by an agreement, that each prelate should erect his crosier in the diocese of the other, and that, while the archbishop of Dublin should be entitled primate of Ireland, the prelate of Armagh should, with more precision, be styled primate of ALL Ireland. But, by a royal patent issued this year, their relative situation was completely reversed, and all the powers and privileges of the primacy of *all* Ireland were conferred on the archbishop of Dublin and his successors. Deeply mortified at this indignity, or apprehensive, perhaps, that it was only a preliminary to further severities, Dowdall abandoned his diocese, and retired to the continent, thus depriving his party of a leader whose station commanded respect. The flight of the prelate being considered by the government as a renunciation of his pastoral charge, his place was soon after filled by doctor Hugh Goodacre. The celebrated John Bale, the determined impugner of popery, and a man of profound erudition, was nominated, at the same time, to the bishoprick of Ossory.

The manner of Bale's promotion was very singular. He had received his education at Cambridge, where he became a Carmelite friar; but being converted to Protestantism by the arguments of Thomas lord Wentworth, he married; and in the reign of Henry VIII. was thrown into prison for preaching against the Romish creed: but being delivered from confinement through the interest of lord Cromwell, he retired to Germany, where he resided for several years, till the accession of Edward VI., when he returned to England, and was presented with the living of Bishop's Stoke. In August, 1552, the king paying a visit to Southampton, Bale rode into the town, which was but five miles distant from his parsonage, though but lately recovered from a dangerous illness. As he passed by the house where the king was lodged, he was noticed by some of the royal attendants, who pointed him out to the young monarch. Edward is said to have instantly expressed his pleasure, that he should fill the vacant see of Ossory. Bale pleaded his poverty, age, and bad health, to excuse himself from undertaking the arduous charge; but all his arguments being overruled, he was forced to repair to Ireland, and, with Goodacre, was consecrated in Christ's Church, Dublin, in the month of February, 1553. Goodacre did not live long enough to render any service to the cause of the Reformation; but on Bale's arrival in Kilkenny, he commenced his mission with a zeal and boldness which kept him in a constant state of insecurity, during the short time of his occupancy.

While the kingdom was thus agitated by religious discord, civil broils also prevailed in various quarters. The factious disorders of Ulster became particularly alarming. The earl of Tyrone, notwithstanding his ample submission to Henry VIII. had resumed the old feeling which he entertained when he pronounced a curse on any of the name of O'Neil, who should ever conform to the English manners, or associate with the Saxons. The province became, about this time, greatly disturbed by violent dissensions in his family. John and Hugh, the legitimate sons of the earl, were incensed at their father for his unjust partiality to his spurious son, Matthew, for whom he had procured the title of lord Dungannon, and declared him his heir; and they accused him with having basely sacrificed the ancient dignity of his house by his submission to the king of England. Stung with these reproaches, the earl resolved once more to sacrifice his allegiance to the vain hope of restoring his family to their ancient consequence. He now made common cause with his sons, John and Hugh, against his late favourite, Matthew; which being communicated by the latter to the lord deputy, the earl and his countess were suddenly arrested and sent prisoners to Dublin.

Incensed at what he pronounced an act of horrible perfidy, John O'Neil declared war against lord Dungannon, to whose assistance the deputy hastened with some newly raised levies.

But O'Neil being reinforced by a body of Scots who had lately made a descent upon Ulster, attacked and defeated Sir James Crofts and his ally, with great slaughter, and spread devastation through one of the most flourishing districts in the island, sixty miles in length, and forty in breadth.

In the midst of this confusion, king Edward VI. died at Greenwich, in the sixteenth year of his age; and the succession of Mary, on the 6th of July, 1553, terminated, for the present, the efforts of the Reformers in both countries. The new queen confirmed all the state officers in their several departments; restored Dowdall to the office of primate of ALL Ireland, and granted a general pardon to all her subjects; but the only change made in religious matters during the first year of her reign, was the issuing of a licence for the celebration of mass, and the royal title of supreme head on earth of the church of Ireland was still inserted in all public acts. The most politic measures were, however, resorted to, in order to prepare the minds of the people for the re-establishment of the Roman Catholic worship; and among other acts of grace, Gerald, the young earl of Kildare, who had been so cruelly persecuted by Henry VIII. was restored to all the honours and possessions of his ancestors. In 1554 he returned to Ireland, in company with Thomas, the young earl of Ormond, and a son of lord Upper Ossory, both of whom had been educated with king Edward VI., and in especial favour with him. Charles Kavenagh, the head of the great Irish house of Mac Murchard, was now elevated to the peerage, by the title of lord Balyan; and O'Connor of Offaley was liberated from his long confinement in London, through the intercession of his daughter, and permitted to return to Ireland. The rights of Gerald Fitzmaurice, lord Kerry, were, about this time, preserved by the singular fidelity of a female, which exhibits, in a striking point of view, the sacred light in which the tie of fosterage was held by the native Irish. Three lords of this name had died within two months of each other. Gerald, the next heir, who was now in his fiftieth year, having been for a long period in the service of the emperor, was at this time in Italy, and another branch of the family seized the opportunity of his absence to take possession of the valuable territory of Lixnaw. But his unjust design was defeated by the zeal and courage of Joan Harman, who had nursed the late lord. Though now nearly eighty years of age, she, with her daughter, sailed from Dingle for France, from whence she proceeded by land to Milan, where she found the rightful heir, and having delivered her message, the faithful domestic almost immediately expired. Lord Kerry returned to Ireland forthwith, and after a contest of two years with the usurper, recovered his estate.

When all the necessary preliminaries were arranged, the pliant St. Leger was again sent over to Ireland, to subvert that form of worship which he had so lately established. Primate Dowdall was armed with authority to deprive archbishop Browne and all the married clergy; but most of them fled from the approaching storm, and their benefices were immediately filled by ecclesiastics devoted to the faith of Rome. Bale, bishop of Ossory, had become particularly obnoxious by his zeal against Popery. He frequently preached to the people at the market cross of Kilkenny, and so boldly assailed the Romish tenets, that upon one occasion it nearly cost him his life; a mob headed by some priests having followed him to his house of Bishop's-court, and murdered five of his domestics before his face. The bishop succeeded, however, in shutting the iron gate, and defended it with the assistance of the remainder of his servants, till the mayor arrived to his rescue with a body of four hundred men. On the death of king Edward, the priests proposed that a solemn mass should be celebrated for the repose of his soul! Bale offered to preach a sermon on the occasion; but this not satisfying the priests, "my troth," said the bishop, "then you must go and seek out some other chaplain, for I am no mass-monger—for, of all occupations, methinks it is the most foolish. For there standeth the priest disguised like one that would show some juggling play, and turning his back to the people, he telleth a tale to the wall, in a foreign language." When the storm of persecution began to rise in Mary's reign, he resolved to fly to Scotland; but his troubles were not yet at an end. The captain of a Flemish man of war entered the ship in which he was about to sail from Dublin, seized the bishop, and plundered him of his money, books, and clothes, and after arriving in Holland, he treated him with great cruelty for several weeks, to compel him to pay a large ransom. Being, at length, liberated, he retired to Basle in Switzerland, where he found sincere friends in Melancthon, Pomeranus, and others of the Reformers; and here he resided till the accession of Elizabeth, when he returned to England; but not wishing to resume his bishoprick, he was promoted to a prebend in the cathedral of Canterbury.

Archbishop Browne being replaced in the see of Dublin by doctor Hugh Curwen, while all the other sees were filled with zealous Romanists, primate Dowdall ordered a jubilee to be observed throughout the kingdom, to return thanks to God for the success of his labours; and on the 1st of June, 1556, the earl of Sussex who had succeeded St. Leger in the viceroyalty, called a parliament for the purpose of repealing all the acts of the late kings Henry and Edward relating to religion. But before the deliberations commenced, a bull was received by the lord deputy from cardinal Pole, the pope's legate, for the reconciliation of the kingdoms of England and Ireland to the holy see. The bull was read by the lord chancellor, kneeling; the houses of lords and commons remaining in the same humble posture, in token of reverence and contrition. After the absolution was pronounced, the whole assembly repaired to the cathedral church, where a *Te Deum* was solemnly chanted, for the restoration of the kingdom to the unity of the church. The parliament now proceeded with zeal and alacrity to restore all matters connected with the church to their ancient footing, and revive all the ancient statutes for the suppressionof heresy.

In July 1546, the earl of Sussex marched to the relief of Carrickfergus, which for several months had been besieged by the Scots under James Mac Donnell. The deputy was accompanied in this expedition by the earls of Kildare and Ormond, with Sir Henry Sidney, who became afterwards so celebrated in the affairs of Ireland. On the 18th the Scots were compelled to raise the siege after a battle in which they were totally discomfited, Mac Donnell himself having fallen by the hands of Sir Henry Sidney.

These operations for repelling the inroads of the foreigners had for some time diverted the attention of the lord deputy from the lawless proceedings of John O'Neil, who still continued to spread desolation through a great portion of the northern province. A stratagem of some of his followers had delivered him from his illegitimate brother and rival, the baron of Dungannon, that unhappy lord having been assassinated while rushing forth from his castle to quell a tumult which had been purposedly raised in its neighbourhood. The old earl of Tyrone dying soon after, John assumed all the dignity of the rightful O'Neil, in defiance of the late lord Dungannon's sons; and he speedily formed an army of four thousand foot and a thousand horse, with which he commenced an expedition against O'Donnel, the chieftain of Tyrconnel, who had refused to submit to his authority.

Dissensions had for some time existed in the

family of this chief, who had been detained in prison for two years by his unnatural son Calvagh, while Hugh, another son, joining O'Neil, had pressed him to undertake this expedition, which, if successful, must have ended in the ruin of his own family. Having entered Tyrconnel, O'Neil pitched his camp between two rivers, and denounced vengeance against all who should resist him: and when informed that the inhabitants were secreting their valuable effects, and driving their cattle into the mountains; " Let them," exclaimed the haughty chief, " drive our prey into the midst of Leinster, or let them hide it in the South, we shall pursue it to the remotest quarter of the island. No power shall protect our enemies, or stop the progress of the prince and sovereign of Ulster."

The common danger had now reconciled the old chieftain of Tyrconnel and his son Calvagh, who resolved on making a vigorous defence.— On the latter devolved the command of their feeble force, which the sage advice of the father enabled him to conduct with success.— " Do not," said Tyrconnel to his son, "attempt with our inferior numbers, to meet the enemy in the field. The camp of O'Neil bears a formidable aspect; but what though it be provided with stores of every kind, and every luxury be exposed to sale as in a regular market, yet the state and magnificence of the enemy may be greater than his precaution — attack his camp by night, and one sudden and vigorous effort may at once disperse our enemies, and free our country."

Calvagh made the necessary preparations for carrying this counsel into instant effect. Two valiant youths offered themselves to the perilous task of entering the enemy's camp at the close of day to spy out their situation. As had been anticipated, they found there so little vigilance that they passed the guards, and mixing with the tumultuous soldiers, made their observations unnoticed. An immense light, emitted from rushes twisted together to the thickness of a man's waist, and dipped in grease, served to render O'Neil's tent conspicuous; and here the chieftain lay, surrounded by sixty of his gallowglasses carrying the battle-axe, and an equal number of Scots armed with sword and target. So unsuspicious were the soldiers of O'Neil, that they even invited the emissaries of Tyrconnel to share their repast; but the latter knew that according to the custom of those days, if they had accepted this hospitality, it would have formed a tie between them and their adversaries, the violation of which would have subjected them to the foulest disgrace. They accordingly declined the courtesy, and hastening to their comrades, related what they had seen, and inflamed them with ardour to surprise the enemy. Calvagh O'Donnel instantly formed his little army into a compact body, burst into the hostile camp, and spreading slaughter and confusion amongst its panic stricken defenders, forced his way to O'Neil's tent. The chief, alarmed at the tumult, suddenly started up, and, finding that his guards had abandoned him, saved himself by a precipitate flight. Accompanied only by the two sons of the revolted Hugh O'Donnel, he swam across a river, and with difficulty reached a place of safety, while his army dispersing on all sides, the troops of Tyrconnel were left in possession of a cheaply purchased victory.—Among the victims of this rout was O'Cahan, the chieftain whose high office it was to throw a shoe over the head of the O'Neil after his inauguration, and who bore the name of Cuinagal, which means 'the antagonist of the strangers.' He accompanied John O'Neil, at the head of a large body of his followers, in their expedition into Tyrconnel: but on the retreat, being abandoned by his forces near Loch-Swillen, and travelling without escort, he fell by the hands of his enemies near his own princely residence of Limavady, a delightful spot on the banks of the Roe. The last chieftain of this family had his castle demolished, and his estates forfeited, in the reign of James I. for his connexion with O'Neil and O'Donnel, in their treasonable practices. The duchess of Buckingham, in the following reign, passing by Limavady, paid a visit to the widow of the unfortunate O'Cahan, whom she found amid the ruins of her once splendid residence, the broken casements stuffed with straw, sitting on her bent hams before a miserable fire of branches, and wrapped in a blanket. Such are the dreadful consequences of civil war, which, besides the miseries it inflicts on the passing generation, often extends its ravages to the remotest posterity.

During the latter years of Mary's reign great progress had been made in restoring the Roman Catholic worship to its ancient splendour; but, happily, while the Protestants of England were suffering the most cruel persecutions, and many of both sexes, high in public estimation for their learning and piety, preferred the most horrible of deaths to the abandonment of their creed, in Ireland not a single individual was molested on account of his religious opinions during the whole of this sanguinary period; nay, many English Protestants found a secure asylum in this country during the whole of Mary's reign, enjoying in private the exercise of the worship which they preferred, through the ministration of the Rev. Thomas Jones, a Welsh clergyman, who, in the succeeding reign, was appointed domestic chaplain to the lord lieutenant.

Whether this forbearance is to be attributed to the more important occupations of the English council, or to the little progress which the Reformation had made in Ireland, it is more than probable that it would have been quickly laid aside, had the sanguinary reign of Mary been permitted to continue. This opinion receives strong confirmation from a story which I shall now tell you, on the authority of the famous archbishop Ussher, the first earl of Cork, and Sir James Ware, the celebrated Irish antiquarian. They tell us, that queen Mary, towards the close of her reign, had determined to extend her persecution of the Protestants to Ireland, and that she signed a commission empowering Sussex, the lord deputy, to carry her design into effect. This commission was entrusted to doctor Cole, the dean of St. Paul's, to be conveyed by him to Dublin, who, having arrived at Chester, in his journey, stopped at an inn, where he was soon waited on by the mayor, a zealous Romanist. Cole, while conversing with the magistrate, in the exuberance of his zeal, took out of his cloak-bag a leathern box, which he said contained a commission to lash the heretics of Ireland. His hostess, who happened to be a Protestant, having a brother, named

John Edmonds, resident in Dublin, who also professed the same creed, overheard the conversation, and while the doctor was complimenting the mayor down stairs, she seized the opportunity to open the box, and taking the commission out, she put in its place a pack of cards, with the knave of clubs uppermost. On returning to his apartment Cole put up his box, without suspecting the trick, and on the next day sailed for Dublin, where he arrived on the 17th of October, 1558. He repaired directly to the castle, and presented the box to the lord deputy in full council, who ordered the secretary to read her majesty's commission; but when the box was opened it was found to contain nothing but a pack of cards. The astonishment of the council at this strange metamorphosis was soon turned into amusement at the learned doctor's expense, who, vehemently protesting that he had actually received the commission, whatever had become of it, was desired by the deputy to return for another, and that, in the mean time, he and the council would shuffle the cards. Cole did as he was commanded, and procured another commission; but being detained for some days by foul weather, queen Mary died before he sailed, and thus was the sanguinary project frustrated. The Protestants considered this occurrence as a singular interposition of Providence; and when lord Sussex related the story to queen Elizabeth, we are told that she sent for Elizabeth Edmonds, the instrument of their preservation, and settled upon her forty pounds a year for life.

CHAPTER VII.

Accession of Elizabeth—John O'Neil assumes the Sovereignty of Ulster—His interview with Sir Henry Sidney—Restoration of the Reformed Worship—Primate Loftus—Creagh, the titular Primate—Discontents—Insurrection in Ulster—John O'Neil in London—O'Neil restored to favour—The Geraldines and Butlers—Battle of Affane—Sir Henry Sidney, Lord Deputy—Mac Arthy More—Hostile Proceedings of O'Neil—Battle of Derry—Destruction of Armagh—Battle of Dundalk—John O'Neil assassinated—Feuds in the South—Desmond arrested and sent to the Tower of London—Vigorous conduct of Sir Henry Sidney—A Parliament—Attainder of John O'Neil.

WE have now arrived at a reign which is justly considered one of the most memorable in English history, and it should be studied with deep attention by my young readers, because of the important influence it has had on the subsequent affairs of this country. Since the accession of the house of Tudor to the throne of England great efforts had been made to crush the power of the Irish chieftains and their allies of the English race, but it was reserved for the last sovereign of that family, after a long and sanguinary struggle, to give the mortal blow to the feudal system in Ireland, and permanence to that change in the established mode of worship which had been thrice altered in the three preceding reigns.

Elizabeth, the only surviving child of king Henry VIII. ascended the throne of England on the 17th of November, 1558. She was then in her twenty-fifth year, and had in the former part of her life passed through vicissitudes well calculated to mature a judgment naturally strong and discriminating. Her sufferings during the reign of her sister Mary had endeared her to the majority of the nation, and the first act of her administration in appointing Sir William Cecil (afterwards lord Burleigh) to the office of principal secretary of state, evinced the new queen's disposition to re-establish the Reformed worship, which was soon after effectually accomplished in England.— To his wise and vigorous counsels, (under divine Providence) was Elizabeth afterwards indebted for the singular success which crowned her long and eventful reign, surrounded as she was by perils both of a foreign and domestic nature, such as have been rarely surpassed in the history of sovereigns.

Ireland was at this period in a state of comparative tranquillity, though considerable apprehensions were entertained from the movements of John O'Neil, who had again collected his forces after his precipitate flight from Tyrconnel. He now assumed the sovereignty of all Ulster, a claim which was generally acknowledged by his countrymen, to whom he had recommended himself by his bravery, munificence, and hospitality, qualities which have been sufficient in all ages to secure the good opinion of the Irish. His cellars, we are told, never contained less than two hundred tuns of wine or usquebaugh, of which he was himself in the habit of drinking to such excess, that frequently when intoxicated, his attendants placed him chin-deep in a pit, casting earth around him, and in this clay-bath he remained until the velocity of his blood had abated. He still professed a peaceable disposition to the English crown, but his assuming the chieftainry of Tyrone, was considered an act of defiance to the government, which had created his father an earl, and vested him with his lands by English tenure, limiting the succession to his brother Matthew and his issue: and Sir Henry Sidney, who administered the government in the absence of the earl of Sussex, now in England, marching northwards by advice of the council, in January 1559, to repress his arrogance, issued a summons commanding the chieftain to attend him at Dundalk, to explain his conduct, and give security for his loyalty. But notwithstanding the apparent rudeness and simplicity of his manners, John O'Neil was circumspect and acute, and he knew that his authority over his followers depended on the opinion which they entertained of his dignity and power. He therefore declined attending the deputy at his quarters, which might be construed into an acknowledgment of his superiority; but he at the same time expressed in the fullest manner his duty to the queen, and reverence for her governor; and requested that Sir Henry Sidney would honour him with a visit, and become sponsor to his child.

With this request the deputy deemed it politic, under present circumstances, to comply: and after partaking of O'Neil's hospitality, he proposed that they should enter upon the discussion of the chief object of his visit. He found the chieftain fully prepared to defend his conduct. " I have," said O'Neil, " opposed the succession of Matthew's children to the sovereignty of Tyrone, because it is well known that this Matthew, whom Henry VIII. incautiously created baron of Dungannon, was the offspring of a mean woman of Dundalk, the wife of a smith, and for sixteen years reputed to be his son, until earl Con, my father, accepted him as his child, on the allegation of an adulteress, and with a shameful partiality preferred him to his legitimate issue. If I were to resign my pretensions in favor of any son of such a father, one hundred persons of the name of

O'Neil would be ready to start up, and assert the honor of their family against the usurpation of a spurious race. The letters patent (he added) on which this claim is founded, are in effect vain or frivolous; for earl Con, by the ancient institutions of the country, could claim no right in Tyrone, but during his own life, nor could he surrender his tenure without the consent of all the lords and inhabitants of that district, which had not known the English law, nor ever been reduced to an English county. Were it even admitted (he continued) that the inheritance should descend in succession to the rightful heir, I am the rightful heir as eldest of the legitimate sons of Con. But my pre-eminence is derived from an origin still more glorious—from the free choice of my countrymen, who, on my father's death, elected me their chief, as the best and bravest of my family; an election ever practised in this country, without any interference of the crown of England."

The deputy was astonished at the firmness of the chieftain, and being unprepared to combat his reasoning, he, by the advice of his counsellors, told O'Neil, that the points which he had stated were of too great importance for his decision, and that they must be communicated to the queen; but he advised him, in the mean time, to practise a peaceable and dutiful demeanour, and that he might be assured of receiving justice from his sovereign. The chieftain promised to follow his counsel, and the conference broke up with the greatest apparent cordiality.

Towards the close of this year, the earl of Sussex returned to Ireland, to resume the office of chief governor, with the queen's special instructions for restoring the Reformed worship. This nobleman, though nearly related to Elizabeth, by her mother Anne Boleyn, had been much in the confidence of her sister Mary, and some doubts were entertained of his sincere attachment to Protestant principles; yet he now showed no reluctance to overthrow what he had assisted in re-establishing during the late reign. The deputy assembled a parliament on the 11th of January, 1560, for effecting those alterations in ecclesiastical affairs which had already been accomplished in England; and, astonishing to tell, in a few weeks, notwithstanding the violent hostilities which had so long prevailed between the two churches, the whole ecclesiastical system of queen Mary was entirely reversed. Of nineteen Irish prelates who attended this parliament, only Walsh bishop of Meath, and Leverous bishop of Kildare, opposed the restoration of the queen's supremacy over the church, the enforcement of the use of the Book of Common Prayer, and the repeal of the laws against heretics, which had been passed in the late reign; the act for this purpose declaring that no opinions should be accounted heresy, but those which could be proved such, on the authority of the canonical Scriptures.

But notwithstanding the pliant conduct of the bishops, the inferior clergy inveighed loudly against the heretical queen and her impious ministers. Many of the former quitted their parishes, and there not being a sufficient number of reformed ministers to fill their places, the churches fell to ruin, and the people were for some time left without any religious instruction. The primacy, which had continued vacant for nearly four years, since the death of Dowdall, was at length filled up in 1562, by the appointment of doctor Adam Loftus, chaplain to the earl of Sussex, to the archbishopric of Armagh. But the pope, resolved to keep up an uninterrupted succession of Roman Catholic primates in Ireland, had previously nominated doctor Richard Creagh to this high dignity.

Some historians inform us, that the life of this prelate was exposed to very extraordinary vicissitudes. He was the son of a respectable merchant in Limerick, and had in his youth acquired an ardent thirst for literature and Scriptural knowledge. But he afterwards, probably in compliance with the will of his father, engaged in mercantile pursuits which led him to make frequent voyages to Spain. When about to return from one of these expeditions to his native country, he deemed it his duty to repair to church, to seek the divine blessing on his undertaking; and while thus piously engaged, the ship sailed without him. This was a great mortification to young Creagh, as he had considerable property on board: but he afterwards had just cause of gratitude to heaven for the disappointment, when he learned that the vessel and all on board had perished at sea. This providential deliverance so deeply affected him, that he determined to devote the remnant of his life to literature and theology. He kept a school for some time in Limerick, and afterwards repaired to Rome, where he entered the church, and became so distinguished by his writings, that the pope nominated him successor to archbishop Wauchop in the primacy of Ireland. His zeal for the Roman Catholic cause, however, soon rendered him obnoxious to the government; and, for what cause we are not informed, he was imprisoned for five weeks in the tower of London. It is stated by an Irish author, that he was again confined in the same place in 1585, and that during his imprisonment, he was falsely accused by the daughter of his keeper, of attempting to violate her person; but that when the girl appeared to give her testimony at his trial, she was seized with remorse, and acknowledged her perfidy. The archbishop was consequently honourably acquitted, but he died in the Tower a few days after.

DISCONTENTS ABOUT RELIGION. 171

The re-establishment of the Reformed church began now to spread universal discontent throughout the country, which was secretly encouraged by the pope and the king of Spain; while unhappily, no wise measures were adopted for convincing the people of the superior purity of that creed which they were called on to embrace. Every person who neglected to attend the church service on Sunday, was liable to a fine; while in many places the people were as ignorant of the English language, as of that in which the mass was celebrated by their former pastors. No steps were taken to send ministers among them, qualified to address them in their native tongue, and thus they were generally left without any religious worship or instruction. It is not matter of wonder that men thus circumstanced should be inclined to listen to any plan for the subversion of the Reformed creed, of the true nature of which they were left in total ignorance, and which they were taught by those spiritutal guides in whom they placed unbounded confidence, to consider as detestable and impious.

The turbulent chieftain of Tyrone was now

looked up to by the discontented party as their natural leader, and while his countrymen reminded him of the ancient glories of his house, his vanity was appealed to by the emissaries of Rome and Spain, as the chosen champion of the church. Nor was John O'Neil unwilling to listen to language which flattered his ambition, while it fully coincided with the invincible antipathy to the English nation which he inherited from his ancestors, and his determined hostility to the late changes in ecclesiastical affairs. As his father Con was said to have pronounced a curse on all his posterity, in case they should learn to speak English, sow wheat, or build houses; so John, as an equal proof of his aversion to the detested race, styled a castle which he built in an island of Lough Neagh, " *Fuaith-na-gaill,*"—" The abomination of the strangers." He hanged up one of his followers on suspicion of being a spy for the government, and another for having so far degenerated from his native manners as to feed on English biscuit. In the year 1560 he again rushed to arms, ravaged the Pale with fire and sword, and then returning to Ulster, he suddenly poured his forces into Tyrconnel, where he surprised his old enemy Calvagh O'Donnel, upon whom he glutted his revenge by throwing him into chains, and carrying off his wife, whom he afterwards kept as his concubine.

To repress these enormities the earl of Sussex marched from Dublin, in July 1561, at the head of a considerable force, on whose approach many of O'Neil's adherents began to desert his standard. The deputy prudently seized the moment for averting hostilities by negociation, and through the mediation of his kinsman, the earl of Kildare, the Ulster chieftain agreed to repair to London, and submit his cause to the queen's decision. He then attended lord Sussex to Dublin, and was entertained by the deputy for some time; but he delayed his promised visit to the English court until it was hinted to him that a design was formed to seize his person, and send him to London as a prisoner.

Finding that any further attempt at evasion would be useless, O'Neil resolved to present himself to the queen not in the character of a suppliant, but as an independent sovereign. He took his departure in 1562 with a magnificent train of followers, and soon after appeared in the English metropolis, attended by a numerous guard of gallowglasses arrayed in the richest habiliments of their country. Each man carried a battle-axe : his head was bare, his hair flowing on his shoulders ; his linen vest, with long and open sleeves, was dyed with saffron, and the whole was surcharged with short military harness. The people of London were astonished at a spectacle which seemed rather like a procession of the inhabitants of some distant quarter of the globe, than those of a sister island. The queen received the chieftain with great apparent condescension; listened to the pathetic narrative of the wrongs he had endured, which he urged as a plea for his excesses, and expressed implicit confidence in his promises of future loyalty. Of this she afterwards gave the strongest proof by making him several valuable presents, lending him two thousand five hundred pounds, and assuring him of her protection.

The followers of O'Neil considered his gracious reception by Elizabeth as an acknowledgment of his dignity, and the successful result of his mission as the happy termination of a contest between two rival potentates; and for some time after his return the Ulster chieftain acted as a faithful ally of the queen of England. The Hebridian Scots still continuing their ravages in the North of Ireland, he made a vigorous attack upon them, slew M'Connell, their leader, and ultimately expelled them from the country. He still, however, continued to exercise his despotic authority over the neighbouring chieftains; but when Maguire, lord of Fermanagh, Magennis, and other Irish lords complained of violence, through the lord deputy Sussex, Elizabeth laconically replied, "Be not dismayed; tell my friends, if he rebel, it will turn to their own advantage —there will be estates for them that want; from me he can expect no further favour." Enraged at this remonstrance against him at the British court, O'Neil burst impetuously into Fermanagh, where he committed horrible devastations, and drove Maguire from his territories.

During these commotions in Ulster, violent feuds had also broken out between the great lords of the South. Gerald earl of Desmond, having obtained possession of his title and estate in despite of the claims of his elder brother Thomas, whom his father had disinherited, soon began to display all the ambition of his most turbulent ancestors, by encroaching on the rights and possessions of his neighbours, and levying those Irish exactions which were forbidden by law on all persons within the sphere of his authority. In the course of these outrageous proceedings, he became involved in litigation with Thomas earl of Ormond, and attempted to get possession of some of his lands by arms. Ormond collected his forces to repel this aggression, and the two parties met on the 1st of February, 1564, at Affane in the county of Waterford, when a desperate conflict ensued, in which Desmond was defeated with the loss of three hundred men. The earl himself was wounded, and taken prisoner; and as the Ormondians conveyed him stretched out on a bier from the field, one of them asked in a tone of triumph,

"Where now is the great lord of Desmond?" "Where," replied the earl with characteristic spirit, "but in his proper place, still upon the necks of the Butlers." The two earls went soon after into England to submit their disputes to the queen, who effected a reconciliation between them; Desmond promising that he would support the execution of the queen's laws within his jurisdiction, and suppress all Irish customs contrary to good order and civility; and as to the furtherance of religion in Munster, *having no knowledge in learning, and being ignorant of what was to be done in that behalf*, he would aid and maintain whatever should be appointed by commissioners nominated for that purpose. What a proof do the characters of O'Neil and Desmond, the two principal chieftains of Ulster and Munster, afford us of the low state of civilization at that period in Ireland!

In the mean time the earl of Sussex had been recalled to fill the office of lord chamberlain of England; and in 1565 Sir Henry Sidney was appointed to the office of viceroy of Ireland, a station for which he was peculiarly fitted, as much by his personal qualities as by his long acquaintance with the country. Like his predecessor in office, he was allied to the royal family of England, and had been the inseparable companion of king Edward VI. who kept him in close attendance during his long decline, and sealed his friendship by breathing his last sigh in his arms. Nor was he less distinguished as being the father of the renowned Sir Philip Sidney, who fell at the battle of Zutphen, at once the glory of his age and nation.

Much benefit was expected from the wisdom and vigour of the new chief-governor; and to assist him, the office of lord president of Munster was created, to which Sir William St. Leger was appointed. Several of the malcontents in this province speedily notified their submission, and Mac Arthy More went to London, where having surrendered his estate to queen Elizabeth, it was regranted by letters patent with the title of the earl of Clancare. But John O'Neil was still the grand object of the vigilance of government. To keep him in awe, the deputy placed a strong garrison in Derry, under the command of Colonel Randolph, an experienced English officer. Not less enraged at this event as a check to his intended enterprizes, than as intimating a suspicion of his disloyalty, the northern chieftain gave vent to his indignation in the most violent language; and learning, at the same time, the elevation of Mac Arthy of Desmond to the English peerage, he proudly exclaimed, to some English commissioners who were sent to treat with him, "A precious earl! I keep a lacquey as worthy as he. But let him enjoy his new honor. It is not worthy of O'Neil. I have, indeed, made peace with the queen at her desire; but I have not forgotten the royal dignity of my ancestors. Ulster was theirs, and shall be mine. With the sword they won it; with the sword I will maintain it."

He instantly led his forces to the walls of Derry, and bade defiance to the governor. Randolph, with a chivalrous spirit, accepted the challenge, sallied out, and defeated O'Neil with considerable slaughter, but lost his own life in the encounter. The chieftain complained of this as an infraction of his treaty with the queen, and solicited a conference with the viceroy at Dundalk that he might lay before him his grievances. Sir Henry Sidney agreed to this proposition, and attended at the place appointed; but, in the mean time, an accidental explosion of gunpowder destroyed the castle of Derry, and compelled the garrison to evacuate the town. The adherents of O'Neil attributed this event to the holy St. Columcille, who had thus taken vengeance of the sacrilegious profaners of his residence. "An enormous wolf," says an Irish historian, "issued out of the woods, snatched up a burning brand in his teeth, and cast it into the church, which the heretics had converted into an arsenal." The chieftain himself was so elated by this stupendous miracle in his behalf, that he disdained to hold any conference with the deputy; set the English at defiance, and declared vengeance against all who should presume to dispute his title to the sovereignty of Ulster.

Having collected fresh forces, he ruined several castles on the borders of the Pale; and then, to avenge himself on primate Loftus, who had given the government some intimation of his hostile intentions, he marched towards Armagh, and destroyed the city and cathedral. He now despatched emissaries into Munster and Connaught to invite Desmond and the Irish lords of those provinces to unite with him, and, in all the dignity of a sovereign, he sent his ambassadors to the pope and the king of Spain to solicit their aid against the common enemy. But his career of conquest lasted not long ; for while besieging Dundalk, he was attacked by a body of the citizens of Dublin, under Sarsfield their mayor, who, aided by a sortie of the garrison, gave him a total defeat, and compelled him to raise the siege.

Sir Henry Sidney now adopted the most prudent and vigorous measures to reduce this dangerous insurgent, the fame of whose exploits had reached the most remote quarters of the island, and was likely to throw the whole country into a flame. He reinstated O'Donnel, Maguire, and the other northern lords who had been dispossessed by O'Neil, in their respective territories, thus firmly attaching them to the English interests, while he himself took his station on the borders of Ulster at the head of a considerable force. No assistance coming to him from any quarter, this unhappy victim of pride and ambition found himself entirely abandoned to his own resources; and in a desultory warfare of a few months, more than three thousand five hundred of his followers were cut off. The remainder of his shattered forces, unable any longer to endure the complicated miseries of war and famine, deserted his standard; and the late mighty chieftain, now become a fugitive, without hopes or resources, determined to cast himself at the feet of the lord deputy, and implore his mercy.

While preparing to execute this design, his secretary suggested that the English government was so provoked at his long continued opposition, it probably would not receive him to terms, and that it would be more prudent for him to seek the protection of the Scots, now encamped at Clan-hu-boy, under Alexander Oge, who, however he might resent his former conduct in taking his brother Sorley-boy prisoner, was still as much as ever the enemy of the English. O'Neil was ready to embrace any counsel which was likely to save him from the disgrace of submitting to the lord deputy, and sending his prisoner, Sorley-boy, before him to explain his intentions, he set out for the Scotish camp, accompanied by his concubine, the wife of O'Donnel, his secretary, and fifty horsemen.

An English officer, named Piers, was at this time stationed in the neighbourhood to watch the motions of the northerns, and having discovered the object of O'Neil's visit to the Scotish camp, he sought every opportunity of enflaming the resentment of Alexander Oge, its commander, against the man who had slain his uncle, James M'Connell, the late Scotish general; and he succeeded so well, that he was permitted to form a plan of deep revenge.— O'Neil was invited to the camp with the warmest assurances of protection, and on his arrival he and his retinue were hospitably entertained in the commander's tent. The carousal proceeded for some time with apparent cordiality; but at length the Scots grew captious and passionate. Mac Gillespie, a nephew of the late general M'Connell, asked O'Neil's secretary if he had not spread a report that his aunt had offered to marry the murderer of her husband. The secretary aknowledged the charge, adding, that the queen of Scots herself might be proud to match with O'Neil. Mac Gillespie gave him instantly the lie direct, upon which the chieftain espoused the quarrel of his secretary. A scene of terrible confusion now ensued, during which Alexander Oge marched in with a body of soldiers, and massacred O'Neil, with his secretary and nearly all his attendants. The mangled corpse of the chieftain was carried to a neighbouring church yard, where, wrapped in a kern's old shirt, it was ignominiously buried; but it was taken up four days after, by Piers, who severed the gory head from the body, which he delivered pickled in a pipkin to the lord deputy, on the 21st of June, 1567, and it was immediately placed on the top of the castle of Dublin: Piers was rewarded for the part he took in this base transaction, with a present of one thousand marks.

Thus was terminated the insurrection of an ambitious chieftain, which had cost the crown of England near two millions of our money, and the lives of about ten thousand individuals. Sir Henry Sidney immediately marched to Tyrone, to compose the disorders of that district, and by the queen's authority he nominated Turlough Lynogh O'Neil, the grandson of that lord who had married into the Kildare family, successor to the chieftainry, and carried the son of the late lord as a hostage to the castle of Dublin.

Fresh quarrels between the Geraldines and Butlers now called the lord deputy into the south. He heard the complaints of the contending parties at Youghal, and reprimanded the earl of Desmond for the devastation he had committed on the lands of lord Ormond, and in various parts of the county of Cork, which Sir Henry Sidney describes in one of his letters, as the pleasantest country he had ever seen; but most miserably wasted and uncultivated, the villages and churches burnt and ruined, the castle destroyed, and the bones of the murdered and starved inhabitants scattered about the fields. Desmond felt so little concern for those devastations, that he told the deputy, who took him with him in his progress, that for one gallowglass which he then kept, he would maintain five, and that before mid-summer he would take the field with five thousand men. But Sidney, resolved to prevent this, carried him a prisoner to Limerick, and from thence to Dublin. He soon after conveyed him to England, where, with his brother, Sir John of Desmond, he was committed to the Tower.

During the absence of the deputy, violent disorders burst forth in all the provinces. The O'Mores and O'Connors again became troublesome in Leinster. In the North, Turlogh O'Neil, after killing in battle Alexander Oge, the murderer of the late chieftain, had united with the Scots to carry on a predatory war against his neighbours. In the South Sir Edmund Butler, brother to the earl of Ormond, was carrying on fierce hostilities with the Geraldines of Munster; and in the same province, James Fitzmaurice, irritated at the imprisonment of Desmond his kinsman, had taken up arms against all who were well affected to the government. Sidney, on his return, proceeded to the North, where Captain Piers had lately defeated the Scots with the loss of two hundred men; and after receiving the submission of Turlogh O'Neil at Carrickfergus, he assembled a parliament at Dublin, with the professed object of restraining the ancient customs and exactions, extending the influence of English law, and making the necessary provisions for the civil and ecclesiastical reformation of the kingdom. In this parliament the government met with violent opposition from the enemies of the Reformed religion, as well as from those who supported their party feuds by Irish exactions, and all who considered themselves neglected by their administration; but after much violent altercation the subsidies were granted, some measures adopted for the promotion of religion and education; and a bill of attainder was passed against the late John O'Neil, which vested his lands and those of his adherents for ever in the crown, and declared that whoever should assume the title of the O'Neil, should suffer all the penalties of high treason: a particular provision, however, was made for Turlogh Lynogh O'Neil and his followers. By this act more than half the lands in Ulster was vested in the queen and her successors.

CHAPTER VIII.

Formation of new Counties—Insurrection of Sir Edmund Butler—Sir Peter Carew—Battle of Kilkenny—Outrages of James Fitzmaurice—Siege of Kilkenny—Siege of Cork—Sir John Perrot President of Munster—Fitzmaurice's Submission—Sir William Fitzwilliam Lord-Deputy—Plantations in Ulster—Sir Thomas Smith—Walter Earl of Essex—Hostilities with Bryan O'Neil—Escape of Desmond—Capture and Execution of Bryan O'Neil—Sir Henry Sidney Lord Deputy—The Viceroy's Progress—Sir William Drury President of Munster—Action with the Desmonians, near Tralee—Death of the Earl of Essex—Insurrection of the Mac-an-Earlas, in Connaught—Grana-Uille.

In the year 1570 Elizabeth had been twelve years on the throne, and during that period a great field had been opened in Ireland for the extension of English law and civility, as it was termed. The district of Annaly was formed into a county by the name of Longford; the greater part of Ulster had become the property of the crown; Connaught was divided into six counties—namely, Clare, Galway, Sligo, Leitrim, Mayo, and Roscommon; and all Irish chieftainries were abolished. Yet no change for the better was effected in the condition of the inhabitants. Each new colony entered the country with the most violent prejudices against the old inhabitants, both of Irish and English descent, while they were viewed by the latter with equal abhorrence, as aliens and intruders, by whom they were excluded from every office of trust and emolument. The petty tyrants of the soil, who were numerous in every quarter of the kingdom, opposed all attempts to introduce a system of liberty and equity—while, on the other hand, the partizans of Rome were with difficulty compelled to yield obedience to a princess, who had been lately excommunicated and consigned to perdition by the Pope, whom they were taught to look upon as her spiritual sovereign.

Various events now concurred to fan the latent spirit of disaffection into a flame. During the late session of parliament, Sir Edmund Butler had been distinguished in the House of Commons by a violent opposition to the measures of the lord-deputy, who openly attributed his conduct to disloyalty. Butler quitted the parliament in a rage, roused his dependents in Kilkenny and Tipperary, and commenced a course of lawless proceedings which fully justified the viceroy's suspicions. Sir Peter Carew, a knight of an ancient and honorable family, had laid claim to some of Butler's lands, and obtained legal authority to take possession of them; but when he attempted to carry it into execution, he was repelled by violence; and when summoned to appear before commisioners appointed to try the case, Butler disdained to obey the mandate.

As the king of Spain had, at this time, an agent in Ireland, named Juan Mendoza, who was secretely practising to excite an insurrection against the government; and as it was discovered that the earls of Thomond and Clancarthy, with James Fitzmaurice, the earl of Desmond's brother, had sent the Roman Catholic prelates of Cashel and Ross to Spain, requiring assistance, Sir. Henry Sidney entertained apprehensions that Butler would unite with them; he, therefore, ordered Sir Peter Carew, who commanded at Leighlin, to reduce him before so dangerous a junction should take place. Carew, being informed that a strong force of the Butlers had assembled near Kilkenny, attacked them with such vigour, that they soon fled from the field, and four hundred are said to have perished in the pursuit.

In the mean time, James Fitzmaurice and his associates had taken up arms, and after committing great devastations in their route, invested the city of Kilkenny. Their tumultuary forces being repelled by the zeal and valour of the garrison and citizens, they wreaked their vengeance on the adjacent country, marking their progress through the most civilized districts of Munster with murder and rapine. They took lord Kerry prisoner, after ravaging his estates; and Sir Warham St. Leger, who commanded in Munster, being at this time in the North, his lady was compelled to shut herself up in the city of Cork, which was speedily invested by the rebel forces. Fitzmaurice, elated by these successes, conceived that the extirpation of the English authority was reserved for his valour, and he sent fresh emissaries to Rome and Spain, to hasten the succours which were to enable him to accomplish an object so successfully begun.

But his project was quickly frustrated by the activity of the lord-deputy, who arriving suddenly to the relief of lady St. Leger, with a chosen body, Fitzmaurice fled to Kilmallock in the county of Limerick, where, after executing the sovereign and several of the principal inhabitants, he set fire to the town. He soon after made his escape to his friends in Ulster, where he concealed himself for some time, and afterwards returned to the South, to raise fresh commotions. The earl of Ormond, having arrived from England, greatly assisted the deputy in restoring peace to Munster. He prevailed on his brother, Sir Edmund Butler, to appear before Sir Henry Sidney at Limerick, and Clancarthy, with all the other great malcontents, were persuaded to return to their allegiance; but the earl of Thomond fled to France, where he fortunately gained the favour of the English ambassador, and, by his mediation with the queen, obtained a pardon, with a pension of £200 a-year.

To accomplish the final reduction of the province to tranquillity, Sir John Perrot was now appointed president of Munster. He was said to be the natural son of Henry VIII. a supposition which received some confirmation, not only from his external appearance, but from his blustering demeanour and coarse language.—Yet he possessed abilities of no common order, and his conduct was marked both by vigour and wisdom, with an anxious desire to improve the condition of the people entrusted to his care. He pursued the insurgents without intermission till he chased them from all their haunts, and compelled Fitzmaurice, their turbulent leader, to make his submission in the church of Kilmallock, where he lay prostrate at the president's feet, who held the point of his sword to Fitzmaurice's heart, in token that his life was at the queen's disposal. While the disaffected were thus terrified, the well-disposed looked up to Sir John Perrot as their protector, who, to complete the pacification of the province, held regular courts for the redress of grievances; and by this firm and judicious course of proceedings, industry and civility appeared to be so generally established throughout the kingdom, that Sir Henry Sidney was permitted to return to England, and the reins of government were entrusted to his brother-in-law, Sir William Fitzwilliam.

This improved state of the country gave rise to many projects among the English, particularly for planting colonies in those parts of Ulster which had become forfeited to the crown. The design was first conceived by Sir Thomas Smith, the queen's principal secretary of state, a man equally celebrated for his talents and his credulity. Having procured a grant of lands in Ulster, his natural son was commissioned to transport a colony into a peninsula called the Ardes, which was considered of easy defence, and here lands were assigned to his followers at the rate of one penny per acre! But young

Smith having been treacherously assassinated soon after by one of the O'Neils, the whole design was frustrated. Yet this failure did not deter Walter earl of Essex from making a similar attempt on a more extended scale. This nobleman, who was a descendant of king Edward III. by a daughter of Thomas of Woodstock, his youngest son, had greatly recommended himself to the queen, both by his learning and valour; and this having excited the jealousy of the earl of Leicester, he was anxious to seek some occupation for him at a distance from the court. Elizabeth, in compliance with his wishes, conferred on Essex half of the district of Clan-hu-boy, comprehending part of the counties of Down and Antrim, on condition of his rescuing the whole of it from the rebels, and defraying half the expenses of the service.

On the 20th of August, 1773, Essex landed at Carrickfergus, accompanied by the lords Dacre and Rich, Sir Henry Knowles, and his four brothers, three sons of lord Norris, who became afterwards distinguished in the Irish wars, and some troops of horse and foot.

Bryan Mac-Phelimy O'Neil, Hugh, lord of Dungannon, with other native chieftains, immediately waited on the earl, to offer their services. But they soon manifested their insincerity, (which is said to have been encouraged by the lord deputy Fitzwilliam) by joining in open rebellion against his authority with Turlogh Lynogh O'Neil the lord of Tyrone. They commenced a system of hostilities of the most annoying description, and so harrassed his forces that the lords Dacre and Rich soon abandoned the enterprise; and the earl himself was on the point of following their example, when his enemies found means to detain him in Ireland, under the pretext of assisting the lord deputy to suppress some commotions which had burst forth in Leinster and Connaught.

In the midst of these troubles, Desmond and his brother, who had been so long detained prisoners in London, found an opportunity for regaining their liberty. Having been freed from their imprisonment in the Tower, under heavy recognizances, they were transmitted to Dublin, to live as state prisoners in the custody of the mayor, who indulged them with such liberty, that, under pretence of hunting, they escaped into Munster, where they were joyfully received by their old followers, who had just at that time received fresh encouragement from Rome and Spain, to persevere in their opposition to Elizabeth's government. Desmond was now proclaimed a traitor, and a reward of one thousand pounds, and forty pounds a year, offered for his apprehension; or half that sum to any person who would bring in his head; but although it was accompanied by a vigorous pursuit by the army, under the earls of Essex and Kildare, Desmond for the present found means to elude all the efforts of the government.

Essex returned from this fruitless expedition to protect his plantation in Ulster from the ravages of his Irish neighbours; and he gained some advantages over them in 1574, taking Bryan O'Neil, the chieftain of Clandeboy, and others, prisoners at Belfast, after an action in which two hundred of the Irish were slain, and their chieftains were afterwards executed at Carrickfergus. A different account of this transaction is given by the historian Leland, on the authority of an Irish manuscript in Trinity College, which states, that after a solemn peace had been concluded between Essex and Bryan O'Neil, the earl invited the chieftain, with a number of his friends, to an entertainment, and that in the midst of their good cheer, Bryan and his friends were arrested, after their followers had been put to the sword before their faces, and being sent off to Dublin, were there hanged and quartered. This barbarous act appears much at variance with the general character of this nobleman; yet it must be confessed that in the unhappy times of which I write, few of the leaders at any side seemed over-scrupulous with respect to the mode of getting rid of an enemy.

In 1575, Sir William Fitzwilliam resigned the Irish government, which was again assumed by Sir Henry Sidney, who instantly proceeded to Ulster, and set up his standard at Armagh, where his presence was sufficient to quell all commotion. He then entered Connaught, and spent a short time in Galway, receiving the submissions of the refractory chieftains of the West, which held good only till his lordship was out of the province; and in the beginning of 1576 he commenced his progress in Munster. The account of this tour, which Sir Henry Sidney sent to the privy council in England, gives a striking picture of the unsettled state of the province and the manners of the people at that period. He praises the loyalty and hospitality of Waterford, where he was entertained with shows both on land and water. The lord Power's country of Curraghmore was remarkable for plenty and good order, because no idlers were suffered there; and though the land was much worse, the tenants made more of one acre than was made of three in the county of Kilkenny. In the Decies, the next district, the case was very different, Sir James Fitzgerald having brought his estate almost to ruin by the encouragement which he gave to idlers. Of the Waterfordians of that day, that quaint and humorous old chronicler, Hollingshed, says, " They are pregnant in conceiving, quick in taking, and sure in keeping. They are very heedy and wary in all their public affairs, slow in the determining of matters of weight, loving to look ere they leap: young and old are wholly addicted to thriving; the men commonly to traffic, the women to spinning and carding—and as they distil the best *aqua vitæ*, so they spin the choicest rug in Ireland."

At Dungarvan the earl of Desmond made a formal submission, and was once more received into favour: this town was found much decayed by Fitzmaurice's rebellion. From a similar cause, the lord deputy found Youghal not able to entertain him and his retinue, which forced him to continue, without delay, his journey to Cork, where he was received with great tokens of joy, and sumptuously lodged for six weeks. This city had greatly improved since it became the residence of the president of Munster, previous to which it was so surrounded with hordes of outlaws, that the inhabitants were forced to watch their gates continually, keeping them shut at meals, and on Sunday during divine service. No stranger was suffered to enter the place with his weapons, and the citizens could take no recreation beyond the walls without being attended by an escort of armed men. In this city the earls of Thomond, Desmond, and Clancarthy, waited on Sir Henry Sidney, with the lords Barry and Roche, and many other lords, and with them a great number of Irish chieftains, as Sir Donald and Sir Cormac Mac-Arthy, whom the deputy recommended the queen to elevate to the peerage; the O'Carrols, O'Regans, Mac-Donoghs, Mac-Fineens, O'Callaghans, O'Driscolls, O'Mahons, and Mac-Swineys, each of whom, said the deputy, had sufficient land to live like a baron or knight in England. They all kept Christmas in Cork, with extraordinary good cheer, expressed their detestation of their former barbarous mode of living, and their willingness to hold their lands of her majesty, and pay her both rent and service. From hence Sir Henry Sidney repaired to Limerick, a city said, even then, to be sumptuously and subtantially builded, where, as he tells the council, he was received with much greater magnificence than he had yet seen in Ireland. Here he was waited upon by the O'Briens and Mac-Briens, the O'Moylans, Bourkes, Lacys, Supples, Purcels, and Red Roches, with the heads of many other great families on the south side of the Shannon, besides the earl of Thomond, the Macnamaras, and others, from the north side, who all complained of what they had suffered during the late troubles, and requested an English force to protect them.

I have been thus particular in tracing the progress of Sir Henry Sidney through Munster, to show you how much that province had improved under the wise and vigorous government of Sir John Perrot. But that brave knight having returned to England in 1576, Sir William Drury, who had served with great reputation as governor of Berwick, was appointed his successor; and such confidence was now placed in the earl of Desmond, that he was nominated one of the council. But this lord became alarmed, when the president signified his determination of extending his jurisdiction into Kerry, which had become the refuge of all the malefactors in the province. Desmond pleaded, in vain, his palatine authority; but, reserving himself for an appeal to the chief governor, he promised all due submission, and invited the president to reside at his house in Tralee. Drury set out soon after, with one hundred and twenty men-at-arms; but, on approaching the town, he was astonished to behold seven hundred of Desmond's soldiers, all tall, active, and vigorous men, advancing upon him. Unacquainted with the customs of the Irish, he at once concluded that he was betrayed, and encouraged his men to make a vigorous onset, rather than suffer themselves to be surrounded and cut to pieces. The Desmonds fled at the first charge; and, the earl being absent, his countess, a Butler of the Dunboyne family, assured the lord-president that these men had not advanced with hostile intentions, but had been assembled by her lord to do him honour, and entertain him with hunting, for which the men of Kerry were greatly distinguished. Sir William Drury appeared satisfied with the explanation, and then proceeded to execute the purpose for which he entered the district.

During these proceedings in the South, the earl of Essex had repaired to England, to lay before the queen the grievances under which he was suffering in Ulster. But the jealousy of Leicester again found a pretext for removing him from court, and he was sent back with the empty title of earl-marshal of Ireland. His future efforts against the Irish were attended with little success, while his spirit was wounded by the intrigues of his court enemies; and these united causes undermining his constitution, he was carried off by a dysentery, in September, 1576.

The ravages of the Mac-an-Earlas (Clanrickard's sons) obliged Sir Henry Sidney, early in 1577, to visit Connaught; and during his residence in Galway, these turbulent youths, to evade the punishment which they dreaded, made a formal submission in the church, and promised in future to be strictly obedient to her majesty's laws. But in less than two months after the lord-deputy's departure, they again flew to arms, by the counsel of the earl their father, crossed the Shannon, and destroyed the town of Athenry, which some workmen were engaged in rebuilding by command of the queen. Then, hiring two thousand Scotish forces, they laid siege to the castle of Loughrea; but this the bravery of the garrison, under captains L'Estrange and Collins, compelled them to abandon, after they had lost six of their principal captains, and one hundred and fifty men. The insurgents then turned their arms against Mac-William Oughter, from whom they took several castles. But the prompt arrival of Sir Henry Sidney put an end to their lawless proceedings;—a great number of them were destroyed in the field, and William, Clanrickard's youngest son, with a son of the earl of Thomond, was hanged at the market-cross of Galway.

There lived at this time, in Connaught, a celebrated heroine, named Grace O'Maley, better known among the Irish as Grana Uille. She was the daughter of Owen O'Maley, whose ancestors, from time immemorial, were lords of a territory stretching from Lough Corrib in the county of Galway to Croagh Patrick in Mayo, and from thence to the vicinity of the town of Sligo, a fine fertile tract, for the most part skirted by the sea and indented by excellent bays and harbours, in which were interspersed many islands of considerable beauty and extent. The O'Maleys, from their maritime situation, had been long conspicuous for naval exploits; and, according to Sir Henry Sidney's report, they were strong in galleys and seamen. The son of Owen O'Maley being but a youth at his father's death, the management of the extensive property of his family both by sea and land devolved on Grace, who, inheriting the spirit of her ancestors, had frequently accompanied her father in his maritime expeditions, and manifested a degree of courage and enterprize unusual in her sex. She had a strong castle in Clare Island, where her larger vessels were moored, while the small craft were kept at Carrick-a-Uille, in the bay of Newport, in the county of Mayo. Here she fixed her residence, and a hole in the castle-wall is still shown, through which a cable was run from a vessel, and fastened to her bed, that she might be instantly alarmed on the approach of an enemy.

Grace O'Maley was first married to O'Flaherty, a powerful chieftain of Connaught, and afterwards to Sir Richard Bourke. She appears to have frequently rendered service to the English, particularly at the battle of Kneilledare, fought by Sir Richard Bingham against a rebellious sept of the Bourkes, where she brought a reinforcement to his assistance at a critical moment, which enabled him to give the enemy a total defeat. For this loyal and zealous conduct queen Elizabeth sent her a letter of thanks, and invited her to court. The invitation was accepted, and Grace O'Maley sailed for England, though far advanced in her pregnancy. She was delivered of a son while on ship-board, called from this circumstance Tibbot-ny-Lung, or Toby of the Ships, who became the first viscount Mayo. She appeared before Elizabeth in the dress of her country. She wore a yellow boddice and petticoat, with a long flowing mantle, while her hair was gathered on the crown of her head, and fastened with a gold bodkin. The queen, surrounded by her ladies, received the Irish heroine in the most gracious manner, and offered to make her a countess; but Grace O'Maley is said to have replied, that as they were both princesses and equals, no honour could be conferred on either by the other; but she accepted the distinction of knighthood for her infant son, who was brought into the queen's presence. Tradition states, that on her return to Ireland she landed in a little creek near Howth, and walking up to the castle, found the gates shut, as the family were at dinner. After making some inquiries, she learned that the infant son and heir of lord Howth was nursing at a short distance; she immediately carried the child on board her ship, as a punishment for the inhospitality she had experienced; nor did she return him till after the payment of a considerable ransom.

Grace O'Maley appears to have had some dispute with the government soon after this; for, in 1579, we find that her romantic castle of Carrick-a-Uille was besieged by a party of the queen's forces, under captain Martin. But the castle was so vigorously defended by this extraordinary woman, that the troops were forced to retreat, after narrowly escaping captivity.

CHAPTER IX.

Traitorous proceedings of Stukeley and Fitzmaurice—Sir William Drury Lord Deputy—Spanish Debarkation at Smerwick—Sir John of Desmond—Murder of Henry Danvers—Death of Fitzmaurice—Duplicity of the Earl of Desmond—Action at Murrow—Battle of Manister—Sir William Pelham Lord Deputy—Desmond and his Brothers proclaimed Traitors—Capture and Recapture of Youghal—The Spaniards at Smerwick put to the Sword—Capture and Execution of Sir James of Desmond—Dreadful State of the Country.

From the beginning of Elizabeth's reign, Spain and Rome had combined their efforts to effect the overthrow of the heretical queen of England; and these courts had now become the resort of every desperate fugitive who could propose any plan for her annoyance. Amongst these was an Englishman, named Thomas Stukeley, who, being obliged to leave his own country for some mal-practices in the reign of Edward VI. had taken refuge in Ireland, where by his enterprising genius he raised himself to some degree of consequence, and even insinuated himself into the good graces of Sir Henry Sidney. But being disappointed in his expectations of becoming seneschal of Wexford, he went to Rome, filled with the most determined aversion to Elizabeth's government. He was introduced by some Irish ecclesiastics to pope Pius V. to whom he extolled the power of the queen's enemies in Ireland, and engaged, with the aid of three thousand Italians, to drive the English out of the country. Gregory XIII. the succeeding pope, cheerfully embraced the overture, on Stukeley's hinting that one of his relatives might be made king of Ireland; and he encouraged Philip of Spain to commence an invasion of the island with the hope that through the valour and address of Stukeley, he would be able to burn the English fleet. A body of eight hundred Italians was soon raised for this service, whom Philip engaged to pay; and the Holy Father was so elevated by the flattering prospects which this adventurer held out, that he assumed the royal dominion of the country, and created Stukeley marquis of Leinster, earl of Wexford and Carlow, viscount Murrogh, and baron of Ross.

James Fitzmaurice was now engaged in the same cause in other parts of the continent. He evinced his gratitude to the queen for the pardon which he received through Sir John Perrot, by immediately repairing to the court of France with Fitzgibbon the White Knight, where he pointed out to Henry IV. the facility with which he might wrest Ireland from the dominion of the English crown. But that monarch, too enlightened to encourage rebellion, advised him to submit to his sovereign, and promised to intercede for him with his good sister Elizabeth. Fitzmaurice, however, rejecting this wise counsel, proceeded to the Spanish court, where he met more attention, and received an introduction from king Philip to the pope, who was soon prevailed upon by two ecclesiastics, Saunders, an Englishman, and Allen, an Irish Jesuit, to sanction his design of invading Ireland: and as these priests consented to accompany the expedition, Saunders was appointed the pope's legate, and Gregory issued a bull exhorting all the prelates, princes, nobles and people of Ireland, to assert their liberty, and defend the Holy Church. It granted the same indulgences to all who should engage in this war as to those who fought against the Turks; and a banner was solemnly consecrated, and delivered to Fitzmaurice, as a chosen champion of the faith.

Stukeley, having embarked his forces at Civita Vecchia, arrived at the mouth of the Tagus at the very moment when Don Sebastian, king of Portugal, was fitting out an armament for the invasion of Morocco. Sebastian promised Stukeley, that if he would accompany him on his expedition to Africa, he would afterwards assist him in the invasion of Ireland; and the unfortunate adventurer consenting, he had the honour of falling with the king of Portugal in that fatal enterprise. This event turned the attention of the Spanish monarch from the conquest of Ireland to that of Portugal, and the apprehensions of Elizabeth being now much allayed, she consented that Sir Henry Sidney should resign the government to Sir William Drury.

Fitzmaurice, in the mean time, had sailed for Ireland, with about fourscore Spaniards, and some English and Irish fugitives, expecting to be speedily followed by the force under Stukeley; and on the first of July, 1579, he landed in Kerry, at a bay called Smerwick. But this had scarcely been effected, when a ship of war from Kinsale, under captain Courtney, doubled the point of land, and cut away his transports. The invaders, undismayed at having their retreat thus cut off, instantly began to raise fortifications on the peninsula, which was hallowed by their chaplains, Saunders and Allen; and they received further encouragement by the speedy junction of Sir John and Sir James Fitzgerald, brothers of the earl of Desmond, with their followers. The earl himself found it necessary, at this time, to temporize; and he even offered to raise forces to attack the invaders; but when the lord deputy pressed the execution of his promise, he found means to evade it on various pretences.

Fitzmaurice and the Spaniards now became alarmed at Desmond's duplicity, and they even expressed doubts of the attachment of Sir John to their cause; but the latter resolved on proving his sincerity by the perpetration of one of the most atrocious actions recorded in the blood-stained annals of our island. Henry Danvers, high sheriff of the county of Cork, an English gentleman of the most benevolent character, had for some time served in this country, and the rectitude of his conduct had acquired for him the esteem and affection of many individuals both of the English and Irish race.— The Desmond family had frequently experienced his good offices; Sir John, in particular, had been repeatedly redeemed from prison by his bounty; and so close was their intimacy, that they generally accosted each other by the familiar appellations of father and son. He was commissioned, upon this occasion, by Sir William Drury, to confirm Desmond and his brethren in their supposed loyalty, and after an ineffectual effort to prevail on them to attack the fort of Smerwick, he set out on his return to the lord deputy. His route lay through Tralee, whither Sir John pursued him with a chosen band of assassins. Having discovered the house which contained his unsuspecting friend, he bribed the porter to leave the gate unbarred, and in the dead of the night, rushed into his chamber with his armed bandits. Danvers, aroused by the tumult, and seeing Sir John, exclaimed, " What, my son, what means this brawl?" But the hardened miscreant only replied by plunging his sword into the breast of his benefactor! His brother assassins, in the mean time, rushing from chamber to chamber, murdered Justice Mead, Mr. Charters, the provost-marshal of Munster, with all their attendants, except an Irish lacquey of Mr. Danvers, who had endeavoured with unavailing fidelity to protect his unfortunate master.

The vile perpetrator of this horrible act returned to the invaders, glorying in the carnage which had sealed his attachment to their cause: yet though he was applauded by the majority, the earl and Fitzmaurice condemned him as guilty of an act of perfidy and ingratitude which no circumstances could justify. But however warmly the foreigners commended Sir John's conduct, they soon became filled with discontent at the non-arrival of the reinforcements which they had been led to expect.— Fitzmaurice, finding it difficult to keep them in subordination, besought them to keep their station, while he should pay a visit to the abbey of Holy Cross, in Tipperary, to perform a vow which he had made in Spain; but his real design was to excite the disaffected in Connaught and Ulster to unite in his cause. Having obtained the consent of his associates, he pursued his route through the county of Limerick, with a small detachment of horse and foot, till ariving on the lands of his cousin Sir William de Bourgho, he ordered his men to seize the first horses they should meet. They accordingly took the horses from a plough belonging to Sir William, upon which the ploughmen set up an alarm, and the knight with his four sons, attended by some kerns, instantly pursued the marauders. They overtook them in a wood, when Fitzmaurice, seeing Sir William's eldest son, thus addressed him, " Cousin Theobald, the taking of garrons shall be no breach between you and me ; if you knew the cause we have in hand, you would assist us :" he then acquainted him with his designs, and the assistance he expected from the pope and the king of Spain. To this de Bourgho replied, " We have too much meddled that way already, and have cause to curse the day when we opposed the queen's authority, and we are resolved never more to swerve from our allegiance." He then demanded that the horses should be returned; and this being rejected by Fitzmaurice, a desperate encounter ensued, in which this turbulent leader with many of his followers were slain, and Theobald de Bourgho, with his younger brother, shared a similar fate. The body of Fitzmaurice was cut up in quarters, and fixed upon the gates of Kilmallock ; and queen Elizabeth rewarded the loyalty of the de Bourghos by creating Sir William lord Castleconnel.

When the Spaniards heard of Fitzmaurice's death, they expressed great anxiety to return to their own country ; but finding all means of retreat cut off, they were compelled to submit themselves to the guidance of Sir John of Desmond, who, abandoning Smerwick, distributed his forces in Kerry, where, through the exertions of the ecclesiastics, their numbers were daily increased, and they were encouraged by the promise of speedy succours from Spain, and a new bull from the pope investing Sir John with the plenitude of his authority. In the mean time Sir William Drury arrived in the county of Limerick with nine hundred men, and issued a proclamation from Kilmallock, commanding all the lords and gentlemen of Munster to repair with their followers to his standard. This was very generally obeyed, and even the earl of Desmond, with well-affected duplicity, joined the lord deputy with a considerable body. It being soon, however, discovered that he maintained a correspondence with the Spaniards, he was committed to custody; yet, with an ill-directed clemency, he was again set at liberty, on renewing his oath of allegiance to the queen.

Sir John of Desmond was now encamped in considerable force near Slievelogher, from whence, for nine weeks, he kept the royal army in constant alarm, and, upon one occasion, cut to pieces a party of two hundred men near Murrow, in the county of Limerick, with their commanders, captains Herbert and Price. The fatigue and vexation of this harassing mode of warfare, overpowered the enfeebled constitution of the lord deputy, who, being seized with a languishing illness, committed the conduct of the army to Sir Nicholas Malby, the president of Connaught, and retired to Waterford.

The success of the rebel leader now filled him with arrogance, and he bid open defiance to the queen's authority: but his exultation was short-lived, for the losses of the royal army were supplied by a reinforcement from England under captains Bourchier and Carew, while Sir John Perrot arrived on the coast with six ships of war to intercept any further assistance from Spain. As soon as his new succours had reached his camp, Sir Nicholas Malby marched from Kilmallock with seven hundred men, and having entered Connello, found the force under Sir John of Desmond drawn up in a plain near an old abbey called Manister-Nenagh. The various dispositions were made by the Spanish officers with a regularity unusual to the Irish; and doctor Allen, displaying the popish standard, gave the strongest assurances of victory. Encouraged by these exhortations, the Irish defended their post for three hours with the greatest obstinacy; but the superior discipline of the English at length put them to flight, after leaving two hundred and sixty men with the famous Doctor Allen dead on the spot.

Malby encamped on the field, and soon after received a congratulatory letter from the earl of Desmond, who, with lord Kerry, had watched the progress of the battle from a neighbouring hill. But some papers which the English commander had found among the baggage of the unfortunate Allen, having convinced him of the earl's dissimulation, he severely expostulated with him on the duplicity of his conduct, and soon after moved his head-quarters to his town of Rathkeal, as a means of securing his obedience. Desmond resented this attack upon his territory by making a fruitless attempt on the English camp. He also put his castles of Askeaton and Carrigfoyle into a posture of defence, which Malby was about to invest when the death of Sir William Drury put an end to his authority in Munster, and he retired to his station in Connaught.

Sir William Pelham was now appointed lord deputy, and having erected the royal standard at Cashel on the 22d of November, he was joined by the earl of Ormond and other well affected leaders with a considerable force, and summoned the immediate attendance of Desmond at his camp. He then proceeded to Limerick, where the mayor presented him with a thousand men well armed, and on the following day, Desmond, with his brethren John and James, and all their adherents, were proclaimed traitors and rebels by sound of trumpet; and a strong force immediately commenced its march to ravage his territories with fire and sword. Desmond retaliated by setting up the standard of rebellion at Ballyhowra, in the county of Cork, and declaring himself openly the champion of the Catholic faith.

He commenced his military operations by investing the town of Youghal, which was speedily surrendered to him by Coppinger, the mayor, who a short time before had refused to admit an English garrison. On receiving intelligence of this event, the earl of Ormond marched to Youghal, and on his way apprehended the traitorous mayor. When he reached the town, he found it entirely abandoned by the inhabitants, not a single person remaining but a friar, whose life he spared on account of the humanity which he had showed in burying the body of Henry Danvers, who had been so basely murdered by John of Desmond. Ormond immediately executed the mayor before his own door, and having issued a proclamation encouraging the inhabitants to return to their dwellings, he left a garrison of three hundred men for their protection.

On the 18th of January, 1580, Ormond was joined by the lord deputy at Waterford, when, dividing their forces, the former captured the castle of Strancally, and devastated the country as far as Slievelogher, putting about four hundred of the insurgents to the sword. Sir William Pelham, at the same time, entered Kerry, and laid siege to Desmond's strong castle of Carrigfoyle, in which he had placed a garrison of fifty Irish and nineteen Spaniards under Don Julio, an Italian engineer. When summoned to surrender, the commander declared that he would defend the place to the last extremity for the king of Spain; and he made a gallant resistance till the breach was stormed by captain Mackworth, when the whole garrison, including their brave leader, were put to the sword. Terrified by this severity, the garrisons of Askeaton and other castles abandoned their posts, and the whole of the surrounding country became a prey to the ravages of the royal forces.

The unhappy Desmond, who had thus, without adequate means or any settled plan of operations, rashly plunged into rebellion, was now become a wretched outlaw. Accompanied by his faithful countess who shared all his misfortunes, his brothers John and James, and his bad adviser doctor Saunders, he wandered in the woods, sending out at night small detachments to procure provisions, or surprise any straggling parties of the queen's troops. In one of these predatory excursions Sir James of Desmond entered Muskerry, and attempted to carry off some cattle belonging to Sir Cormac Mac Arthy. But the prey was immediately rescued by Daniel Mac Arthy, a brother of the knight, after a desperate action, in which one hundred and fifty of Desmond's men were slain, and Sir James himself was mortally wounded. He was found in this state by a blacksmith, a servant of Sir Cormac, who bound him securely, and hid him in a bush till the fight was over, when he conveyed him to Cork, where he was condemned and executed as a traitor, and his head and quarters were fixed on the gates of the city. This unhappy youth perished in his twenty-second year, having been baptized at Limerick in 1558, with great pomp, in the presence of the lord Deputy Sussex.

These terrible disasters excited mutual reproaches between the remaining rebel leaders; and after the countess of Desmond had, upon her knees, sought mercy in vain for her unfortunate husband, Sir John and the legate Saunders resolved to abandon their less guilty associate, and seek refuge with lord Baltinglass and their friends in Leinster. But from this last hope they were cut off by the vigilance of the garrison of Kilmallock, who, after capturing several of their attendants, compelled them to return to Kerry. Had the miseries consequent on this dreadful insurrection, fallen alone on its principals, it would not have been so afflictive to humanity: but their unhappy vassals, bound by the tie of implicit obedience to these imperious lords, were equal sharers in their calamities: and to such misery were they reduced by the ravages of the soldiery, that when bereft of all means of support by the seizure of their cattle, they were seen following the army with their wives and children, entreating the soldiers to rescue them by the sword from a still more horrible death by famine. How dreadful are the effects of civil war! How should the ambitious chief or aspiring demagogue pause before he plunges his countrymen into its vortex. The aggressions of foreign nations are met with a kind of courteous hostility, but the word *rebel* steels every heart to compassion, and appears to justify the most rigorous severities on the part of the ruling power.

CHAPTER X.

Arthur Lord Grey, Lord Deputy—Battle of the Seven Churches—Death of Sir Francis Cosby—Dorcas Sidney—Death of Sir Alexander Cosby and his Son—Fresh arrival of Spaniards in the South—Repulse of the Earl of Ormond at Fort de l'Or—Sir Walter Raleigh—Capture of Fort de l'Or—Recal of Arthur Lord Grey—Exploits of Sir Walter Raleigh—Capture and Death of Sir John of Desmond—Assassination of Gerald Earl of Desmond—Sir John Perrot, Lord Deputy—Popularity of his Government—Scotch invasion of Ulster repelled—A Parliament—Confiscation of Desmond's Lands—Plantation of Munster—Commotions in Connaught—Disputes between the Viceroy and Sir Richard Bingham—Defeat of De Bourgho.

At the moment when the desperate state of Desmond's affairs gave hope that the commotions in Munster were near their termination, Sir William Pelham was suddenly recalled to Dublin, to surrender the sword of state to Arthur lord Grey, who had been appointed his successor, with peremptory orders to shorten the war by a vigorous prosecution of the rebels. Sir William, after leaving the command of the army in the South, now amounting to 3,000 men, with Bourchier, a son of the earl of Bath, pursued his route to the capital by easy journeys: but, before his arrival, lord Grey, impatient for action, engaged in an enterprize which was attended with no common disaster. Soon after his landing, he received intelligence that lord Baltinglass, one of the Fitzgeralds, and Phelim M'Hugh, the chieftain of the O'Byrnes, had taken their station in the valley of Glandelough, or the Seven Churches, in the county of Wicklow, from whence they committed terrible outrages on the surrounding country. He expressed his indignation that such an ignoble enemy should be permitted thus to set the royal government at defiance, within twenty-five miles of the capital; and notwithstanding the wise remonstrances of some veteran officers by whom he was surrounded, he peremptorily commanded them to collect their companies, and drive these rebels from their retreat. They obeyed with an honourable submission, though sensible of the imminence of the danger, and marched boldly to the attack; but as they advanced they met with difficulties almost insuperable, being sunk at one time in the yielding soil, and at another forced to clamber over precipices which disordered their march. While thus pursuing their route through a marshy valley, winding irregularly between hills thickly wooded, they were thrown into disorder by a sudden volley from an unseen enemy on either side, which was repeated with such terrible execution, that soldiers and officers fell in heaps without having any opportunity of displaying their valour. The shattered remnant with difficulty effected their retreat, and lord Grey, who, with the earl of Kildare, and Wingfield the engineer-general, awaited the event on a neighbouring eminence, accompanied them to Dublin, covered with confusion and disgrace.

In this rash adventure fell Sir Peter Carew

the younger, captains Audley and Moore, with Sir Francis Cosby, the general of the Irish kerns, for so our native foot-soldiers were at that time called. Sir Francis Cosby had been much distinguished in the wars of the Low Countries during the reign of Henry VIII. and afterwards married a daughter of protector Somerset. Having got a command in the army of Ireland, he defended the Pale with great bravery against the O'Mores of Leix, and was rewarded by queen Mary with the office of general of the Irish kerns. Elizabeth conferred on him the authority of executing martial-law on all rebels at his own discretion, a privilege which, according to our Irish annalists, he exercised with so little clemency, that a gibbet near his castle of Stradbally, in the Queen's County, was rarely without a tenant. The hostility between his family and the O'Mores was kept up for many years after his death. In 1589, his successor Alexander was treacherously seized by Rory O'More at a conference, and bound to a tree, from which he was rescued by some of his friends, after a sharp encounter. This was fully avenged afterwards, as the knight put to death without mercy such of the insurgents as fell into his power. By his lady, who was a cousin of Sir Henry Sidney, and a favourite of queen Elizabeth, he obtained great tracts of land in the Queen's County. She was a woman of masculine spirit, and her pride of family was such that she never assumed her husband's name, but always signed 'Dorcas Sidney.' The whole of Sir Alexander Cosby's life appears to have been passed in constant hostility with the insurgent O'Mores, which at length terminated fatally for him and his eldest son. On the 19th of May, 1596, Otterburn, a rebel chieftain, demanded a passage over Stradbally-bridge, which being considered by Cosby as a challenge, he resolved to oppose the passage. He accordingly, accompanied by his eldest son Francis, who had lately married a lady of the Hartpole family, took post with his kerns at the bridge, while Dorcas Sidney and her daughter-in-law seated themselves at a window of the abbey to see the fight. The O'Mores soon advanced with great intrepidity, and were resisted with equal bravery, till Sir Alexander Cosby was slain, when his kerns instantly gave way; and Francis, attempting to escape by leaping over the battlements of the bridge, was in the next moment shot dead. You might expect that the ladies at the window now became frantic with grief at the death of their husbands. But no such thing; the widow of Francis turned to her mother-in-law, and said with the greatest self-possession, " Remember, mother, that my father was shot before my husband; and therefore the latter became the legal possessor of the estate, and consequently I am entitled to my thirds or dowry." The ladies now precipitated their flight, but they had scarcely left the abbey when the O'Mores rushed in, murdered all the inmates that remained, and plundered the house of every thing valuable. William, the infant son of Francis Cosby, was secreted by his nurse, but dying soon after, he was succeeded by his uncle Richard, who, in 1606, avenged the death of his father and brother, in a pitched battle which he fought with the O'Mores in the glen of Aughnahely, under the rock of Dunamase. Thus, in those unhappy times, was the spirit of vengeance transmitted from father to son, and the strife of contending parties continued from generation to generation!

Lord Grey had scarcely recovered the shock of his late disgrace, when he received the alarming intelligence that the Spaniards, in the absence of admiral Winter, who had been driven from his station by boisterous weather, had landed seven hundred men at Smerwick, with five thousand stand of arms, and a large sum of money for the use of the insurgents in the south; that they instantly proceeded to complete Fort de l'Or, or the Golden Fort, which their countrymen had begun—and that they expected the speedy arrival of further succours. The earl of Ormond, who commanded in Munster, marched against the invaders, who, terrified at his approach, suddenly abandoned their post, and retired, under the guidance of their Irish auxiliaries, to the wood of Glengalt. But when they discovered the smallness of Ormond's force, they recovered from their panic, and three hundred of them, with their commander, returned to the fort, from whence they made a successful sally, which compelled the earl, who had neither artillery nor provisions for a siege, to retire to Rathkeal, where he was soon after joined by lord Grey, with eight hundred veteran troops, under Sir Walter Raleigh and other distinguished commanders.

Raleigh, who first taught the Irish the use of potatoes and tobacco, was the younger son of an ancient and respectable family in Devonshire, and had acquired some celebrity at the university of Oxford, before his love for military glory induced him, at the age of seventeen, to join a band of volunteers, which his relative, Henry Champernon, led in 1569 to the aid of the French Protestants. In that country he served an apprenticeship of six years to the art of war, and subsequently accompanied the English forces, under Sir Henry Norris, to assist the Dutch. In 1579, a new kind of ambition seized the mind of this enterprizing youth: he attended that gallant navigator, Sir Humphry Gilbert, who was his half-brother, in his unfortunate expedition to

Newfoundland, and after his return he joined the army about to proceed to Ireland under lord Grey, who brought with him, as his secretary, the not less celebrated Edmund Spenser, the poet.

As admiral Winter had by this time returned to his station, the Golden Fort was now invested both by sea and land, and the foreigners were summoned to declare for what purpose they were sent, and why they presumed to erect fortifications in the queen's dominions? The Spanish governor boldly replied, that they were sent by the pope and the king of Spain, to extirpate heresy, and take possession of the country for king Philip, in whom the Holy Father had vested the sovereignty of Ireland, and they seconded this answer by a vigorous sally, which was, however, repulsed. Batteries were now raised against the fort; but before they began to play, the Spaniards were again summoned, with an offer of money if they surrendered; they still replied that they would maintain their post, and endeavour to extend their conquests. A furious bombardment then commenced, which so terrified the commander, San Joseppo, that he offered to capitulate; but lord Grey haughtily replied, that he would grant no terms to traitors or their abettors, and continuing inexorable, the garrison was compelled to surrender at discretion.—They were instantly disarmed, and while the Irish in the fort were reserved for execution by martial-law, the Spaniards, with the exception of their commander and a few officers, were butchered on the spot in cold blood, by a party of soldiers, under the command of Sir Walter Raleigh, who, it is said, was compelled to execute this horrible commission, on pain of being punished for disobedience. Queen Elizabeth is reported to have expressed her displeasure at the barbarous execution; but lord Grey attempted to justify the measure, by saying that as the garrison could show no commission from the king of Spain or the pope, they were to be considered as only private adventurers, who could expect no advantage from the law of nations; that fifteen hundred Irish were approaching, and that no shipping was prepared for the reception of the prisoners.

The news of this invasion having excited the flame of insurrection in the other provinces, lord Grey, after demolishing Fort de l'Or, left the conduct of the army in Munster to the earl of Ormond, captain Zouch being appointed governor of Kerry, and Sir Walter Raleigh to command in Cork. The lord deputy had no sooner arrived in the capital than he was alarmed with reports of a secret conspiracy against the government, in which were implicated the earl of Kildare, lord Delvin his son-in-law, and Nugent, a baron of the Exchequer. The latter, though a man of high character, was executed, notwithstanding his most solemn protestations of innocence; and the two former were sent to England, where, after a solemn investigation of the charges against them, they were acquitted of every suspicion of disloyalty, while Grey's administration was proved to be attended with such tyranny and barbarity, that little was left for the queen to reign over in Ireland but ashes and carcasses. He was soon after recalled, and Loftus archbishop of Dublin, and Sir Henry Wallop, were appointed lords justices.

Munster, in the mean time, was governed with rigour; and a watchful eye was kept on all the great lords of the English race, who still adhered to the Roman Catholic creed, and refused to furnish aid to the queen's service. Hence arose many petty skirmishes and feats of arms, in which Sir Walter Raleigh proved himself a distinguished partisan. Upon one occasion he was commissioned to seize the castle of Barry's-court; but lord Barry having intimation of his approach, set it on fire, while the seneschal of Imokilly, set an ambush at a place called Chore-abbey, near Middleton, to surprize Raleigh on his return. The knight had with him only six horsemen and a guide, and having outridden his men, he arrived alone at a ford, where he was perceived by the seneschal, who put spurs to his horse, and crossed him in the water. Raleigh, however, gained the opposite bank; but being forsaken by his guide, he was left alone, with his staff in one hand, and a cocked pistol in the other, in view of the seneschal and his party, who not venturing to attack him, the passage of his men was secured.

Soon after this he routed David Barry, who was at the head of several hundred rebels near Cloyne; and lord Roche being suspected of corresponding with the insurgents, he was ordered to bring him and his lady to Cork. Raleigh set out at ten o'clock at night with ninety men: before morning he reached Ballynaharsa, the house of lord Roche; and though five hundred of the neighbouring peasantry flew to arms at his approach, he obtained an entrance with six chosen men, while the rest of his party guarded the gates. He was received by his lordship with great hospitality; but after dinner, Raleigh informed his host, that the painful duty was imposed upon him of conveying him and his lady to Cork. Roche, finding remonstrance fruitless, obeyed, and with his lady set out for Cork during a dreadfully tempestuous night, which proved fortunate for Raleigh's small force, as his old friend the seneschal was thereby prevented from attacking him with a body of eight hundred men whom he had assembled for that purpose. Lord Roche, however, was honourably acquitted of the charges preferred against him, and afterwards distinguished himself as a loyal subject.

In the beginning of 1581, the English garrison of Cork made a capture of much greater consequence. Zouch, the governor, having received intelligence that a quarrel had arisen between lord Barry and the seneschal of Imokilly, and that Sir John of Desmond was expected on a certain day at Barry's camp to reconcile them, left the care of Cork to Raleigh, while he, with captain Dowdal, set out with a party of soldiers for Castle Lyons. On their arrival, they posted their musketeers between a wood and a bog, and a few minutes after, they perceived two horsemen, who proved to be Sir John of Desmond, and Fitzgerald of Strancally. They were quickly surrounded and made prisoners; but not till Sir John, the base murderer of Henry Danvers, had been mortally wounded. He died on his way to Cork; but his body was hanged by the heels on a gibbet, and his head was sent to Dublin, and placed on the castle. Fitzgerald of Strancally was also executed; and Barry's army being put to the rout, that chief was compelled to sue for pardon.

The wretched Desmond was now reduced to the most dreadful extremities. His brothers had perished by the hands of their pursuers; and his adviser Saunders, the pope's nuncio, the prime cause of all his misfortunes, after wandering for two years in the woods, a wretched fugitive, was found dead and mangled by beasts. In the beginning of 1582, the lords justices once more invited Desmond to return to his allegiance; but still, unsubdued by his misfortunes, he is said to have impiously replied, ' that he would rather forsake God than his men.' He now wandered for many months in the woods of Limerick and Kerry, generally destitute of common necessaries, and often experiencing hair-breadth escapes. At the Christmas of this year he was lurking in the wood of Kilquaig, near Kilmallock, when his place of shelter was attacked by some soldiers, who slew his servants, and carried off some booty; but he and his countess escaped almost naked, and saved themselves by standing up to the neck in a river under a bank till their pursuers had departed, In August, 1583, he was in the wood of Aharlow with sixty of his gallow-glasses or troopers, who, while cooking some horse-flesh, were suddenly attacked, and the greater part put to the sword; their wretched master being indebted for his preservation to the fleetness of his horse. He now threw himself on the protection of one Gowran M'Swiney; but he was soon deprived of this support, M'Swiney being slain while returning from a predatory excursion into Carberry. Kerry was his next place of refuge; and here he lay concealed for some time, with a few trusty servants, in a wood near Tralee, compelled to support himself and his followers at the expense of the neighbouring peasantry. Among various depredations committed by them, some cattle were taken from a poor woman named Moriarty. She complained to her brother, who applied to the English governor of Castlemain for assistance. The governor granted him seven musketeers and twelve horsemen, under the command of one Kelly, an Irishman, who followed the track of the cattle, till they came to a wood four miles east of Tralee, where they resolved to take up their quarters for the night; but perceiving a fire not far off, they advanced towards it, and discovered six persons sitting in a ruined house. They all fled at the entrance of the soldiers, except an old man, whom Kelly struck with his sword, and nearly cut off his arm; upon which his wretched victim exclaimed, "Spare my life! for I am the earl of Desmond." But finding that the earl would be unable to travel from loss of blood, his executioner bade him prepare for death, and then struck off his head, which was sent to England, and fixed upon London bridge. Kelly was rewarded for this service with an annual pension of £20, but he was afterwards hanged at Tyburn.

In this manner was terminated the turbulent career of Gerald the sixteenth earl of Desmond, who, by joining in an ill-concerted scheme of rebellion, in which he was unable to make one distinguished effort, deprived his posterity of those princely domains in which his family had, during four centuries, exercised all the rights of sovereignty. His prodigious estates in Cork, Kerry, Limerick, and Waterford, extended one hundred and fifty miles, and contained five hundred and seventy-four thousand six hundred and twenty-eight acres, on which were numerous flourishing towns and strong castles. He was able to take the field with several thousand men; and of his own kindred and surname he could reckon five hundred gentlemen.

The complete suppression of the rebellion in Munster afforded the English government an opportunity to model the country on liberal and equitable principles. But some of Elizabeth's counsellors appear to have been actuated by a base jealousy of Irish prosperity; and they openly avowed their apprehensions in the English parliament, that if Ireland were reduced to order, and the wealth and consequence of the people increased, they would speedily cast themselves into the arms of some foreign power—a horrible system of policy, which was strongly reprobated both by Sir Henry Sidney and Sir John Perrot. The southern province was nearly depopulated by the late rebellion, and now exhibited a terrible spectacle of famine and desolation. Desmond's lands were to be parcelled out to new tenants; and various other regulations were contemplated, which required that the reins of government should be entrusted to a firm hand; and the appointment of Sir John Perrot to the office of viceroy was hailed with joy by all classes of the inhabitants, so deeply were they impressed with a sense of the vigour, justice, and impartiality with which he had conducted his government of Munster.

He commenced his administration in June, 1584, by publishing a general amnesty to all who would return to their allegiance; and he set out soon after on a tour to the different provinces. In Connaught his presence intimidated the turbulent de Bourghos, and he placed the whole province under the presidency of Sir Richard Bingham. The Irish chieftains of Ulster crowded round the viceroy with the loudest professions of loyalty, and seven new counties were formed in that province. On his return to Dublin he assembled a parliament, at which some Irish lords and knights attended; and Sir John Perrot felt not a little pride that he succeeded in persuading them to lay aside their national dress, and conform to the manners of the court. Yet they manifested considerable reluctance; and when Turlogh Lynogh O'Neil, earl of Tyrone, appeared in his old age, dressed in his fashionable habiliments, he expressed his discontent with a good humoured simplicity—" Prithee, my lord," said he to the viceroy, " let my chaplain attend me in my Irish mantle, then shall your English rabble be diverted from my uncouth figure, and laugh at him." The Irish lords of Thomond, Clancarthy, Inchiquin, and Upper Ossory, also attended this parliament; and some of the members of the House of Commons belonged to the native families of O'Brien, O'Reilly, O'Farrell, Mac Brien, and Mac Gennis.

As great alarm existed at this time of a foreign invasion, Sir John Perrot was called into Ulster, by the arrival of a considerable force from Scotland, under Alexander Mac Donnel, the son of the famous Scotch chieftain Sorleboy. But before the arrival of the deputy these troops were totally defeated, and their captain executed as a traitor, as he had formerly sworn allegiance to the English government. Perrot had therefore only to receive submissions and hostages from those chieftains who were suspected of disaffection. Even the old Scotish chieftain Sorleboy attended, and renewed his engagements. Upon this occasion an Englishman had the mean brutality to insult the unhappy father on the late misfortune of his son, and to point exultingly to his head which was erected on a pole at no great distance. The brave old Scot viewed the terrible spectacle with stern composure, and casting an indignant look upon his insulter, calmly said, "*My son hath many heads!*"

After the suppression of this commotion, the viceroy returned to Dublin, and immediately commenced the most praiseworthy efforts to procure the complete pacification of a country which had suffered so much from turbulence and ill-government, by a policy at once vigorous, impartial, and benevolent.

In the session of parliament which assembled in 1586, bills of attainder were passed against the late earl of Desmond and one hundred and forty of his adherents, and all their estates, amounting to near six hundred thousand acres, were declared forfeited to the queen. This enabled Elizabeth to accomplish her favorite project of establishing an English colony in Munster: these lands were accordingly divided into seignories of from twelve to four thousand acres each, for which the undertakers were to pay the annual rent of three pence per acre, settle upon them a prescribed number of English families, and furnish the state when required with a certain number of soldiers. Among the principal undertakers was Sir Walter Raleigh, who had made so distinguished a figure in the late civil wars of the south. A quarrel with lord Grey had retarded his promotion in Ireland, and when that nobleman was removed from the viceroyship, he followed him into England, and found means to have their dispute brought before the privy council. The talents and eloquence with which Raleigh pleaded his own cause upon this occasion, raised the admiration of his audience, and proved the means of introducing him to the presence of the queen, in whose good graces he rose with extraordinary rapidity. He now became the frequent companion of her majesty's walks, and it is recorded that when upon one of these occasions she reached a miry spot, and stood in perplexity how to pass, Sir Walter, whose only fortune at that time consisted of a respectable wardrobe, adroitly pulled off his rich plush cloak, and threw it on the ground to serve her for a foot-cloth. The queen graciously accepted this flattering attention, and it was afterwards wittily observed, that the spoiling of Raleigh's cloak had gained him many *good suits*. It assisted in obtaining for him forty-two thousand acres of Desmond's lands in Cork and Waterford, including a great part of the town of Youghal, where he resided for some years, and planted the first potatoes that were grown in Ireland. The house which he inhabited still remains, and for a long period it was preserved in the same state in which it was left by its illustrious occupant.

The late introduction of English law into Connaught began about this time to excite a very general disposition to rebellion in that province, through the turbulence of some degenerate branches of the de Bourgho family. Sir Richard Bingham, the president, with the newly appointed sheriffs, had resolved to punish every symptom of insubordination with the utmost severity; and in some counties they are said to have acted with a degree of arbitrary cruelty, which excited a very general aversion to the new system. Thomas Roe de Bourgho, having refused to attend the sessions of Mayo, was ordered to be seized by Sir Richard Bingham. In resisting the order he was killed, and two of his adherents being taken, were executed. This vigorous conduct of the president filling the whole sept of the de Bourghos with terror, they made such representations to Sir John Perrot, as called forth a censure on Bingham's conduct. The de Bourghos were encouraged by this to new acts of insubordination; and while Bingham was employed in besieging the castle of Clanowen in Clare, which was defended by Mahon O'Brien, a noted outlaw, they fortified themselves in the castle of Lough Mask, strongly situated on the borders of a lake in the county of Galway, and bade defiance to the power of the English. Bingham, after having taken Clanowen, and slain O'Brien, advanced to Lough Mask, upon which he made a fruitless assault by water, which was the only mode of access, several of his men and boats having perished in the attempt. The garrison, however, being apprehensive of a more powerful attack, abandoned the fortress, and Richard de Bourgho, one of their principal leaders, surrendered himself to the president, who, contrary to the orders of the lord deputy, ordered him to instant execution.

Sir John Perrot, irritated by the arbitrary proceedings of the president of Connaught, issued his mandate that he should grant protection to all who submitted. Bingham obeyed, and then repaired to Dublin to give an account of his proceedings to the privy council. A violent altercation now took place between the deputy and the president, the former accusing the latter of injustice and oppression, while Bingham defended his own conduct by the plea of necessity. The opinion of the president received confirmation by the arrival of intelligence that the de Bourghos had thrown off their allegiance to the queen, declared for Spain and Rome, and commenced a new scene of outrage. Bingham being once more entrusted with the conduct of the war in this province, marched towards Ballinrobe, where he was joined by the earl of Clanrickard, lord Athenry, with O'Kelly and other Irish chieftains. He first endeavoured by negociation to bring the de Bourghos back to their allegiance, but this proving fruitless, he executed their hostages which he held in his hand, and then pursuing them into their retreats, drove them in a few weeks to a state of desperation, from which, however, they were for a moment recovered by the junction of two thousand roving Scots, who landed on the coast of Sligo. These, with some troops brought to their assistance by Sir Arthur O'Neil and Hugh Maguire, increased their force to more than three thousand. Sir John Perrot, on receiving this alarming intelligence, marched towards the western province; but before his arrival, Bingham, with the aid of some of the Irish clans, had attacked the enemy, destroyed two thousand of them, and thus terminated the rebellion in Connaught. General tranquillity appearing now to be established in the country, the English government was encouraged to withdraw a great part of the regular forces from Ireland, for the service of the Netherlands—a measure which obliged the lord-deputy to convert the natives, in many places, into a standing militia, by which they were instructed in the use of arms, and fitted to bear a prominent part in the transactions that will be recorded in the following chapter.

CHAPTER XI

Discontents in Ulster — Character of Hugh O'Neil — He obtains the Earldom of Tyrone — Treacherous Seizure and Imprisonment of Red Hugh O'Donnel — Recal and Death of Sir John Perrot — Sir William Fitzwilliam, Lord Deputy — The Spanish Armada — Wrecks on the Irish Coast — Kind reception of the Spaniards by the Natives — O'Ruarc and Don Antonio de Leva — Avarice and Cruelty of the Viceroy — Tyrone's Dissimulation — Escape and perilous Adventures of Red Hugh O'Donnel — Tyrone's Outrages — Sir William Russel, Lord Deputy — Maguire of Fermanagh — Action at Sciath-na-Feart — Death of Archbishop Magawran — Exploits of O'Donnel — Siege of Enniskillen — Action at the Ford of Biscuits — Devastation of Connaught — Tyrone commences Hostilities — Sieges of Portmor and the Castle of Monaghan — Sir John Nor-

ris—*Battle at the Pass of Cluain-Tibhin—Terrible Conflict between Tyrone and Sedgrave—Conference and Armistice with Tyrone and O'Donnel—Renewal of Hostilities—Action at Killoter—Capture of Armagh by a singular Stratagem—Temporary submission of the Ulster Chieftains—Sir Conyers Clifford, President of Connaught—Death of Sir John Norris—Thomas Lord Borough, Lord Deputy—Fresh Hostilities—Defeat of Sir Conyers Clifford at Tyrrel's Pass—Exploits of O Donnel in Connaught—The Viceroy defeats Tyrone near Armagh—Death of Lord Borough and the young Earl of Kildare—Tyrone's Conference with the Earl of Ormond—Sir Henry Bagnal marches to the relief of Portmor—Surprise of Tyrone's Camp—Battle of the Yellow Ford—Death of Field Marshal Bagnal, and decisive Defeat of the Royal Army.*

THE late introduction of the English polity into the province of Ulster was speedily productive of alarming commotions, through the tyrannical proceedings of the sheriffs and other officers of the newly-formed counties. Sir John

Perrot being unable to send any forces for the maintenance of tranquillity in this quarter, the Irish lords became less cautious in expressing their abhorrence of the English government, to which they were now encouraged by the vast preparations making in Spain for the invasion of England. Among these stood conspicuous Hugh O'Neil, the son of that Matthew, who, though the illegitimate son of Con *Baccagh*, earl of Tyrone, had been created lord Dungannon by Henry VIII. Hugh O'Neil was a man of no common order, and had times or circumstances proved equally propitious, he might have stood in the same rank with some of our most celebrated military leaders. He had entered early in life into the service of Elizabeth, and commanded a troop of horse during the hostilities in Munster, being admirably fitted by nature for desultory warfare and hazardous exploits. He possessed a vigour of constitution capable of enduring the severest privations. He was brave, vigilant, and temperate, and with these advantages were united great acuteness of intellect, which had been improved by a liberal education, the most polished manners, and unremitting industry. Yet he was such a perfect master of the art of dissimulation, that among his own people he could completely conceal this refinement, and assume all the barbarous manners of his ancestors.

Hugh O'Neil had petitioned the Irish parliament, during its late session, that he might be restored to the title of earl of Tyrone, with the inheritance annexed to it, in virtue of the grant to his grandfather, earl Con, to his father and his heirs. The title was readily granted; but the inheritance having been forfeited to the crown, by the attainder of the late John O'Neil, the claimant was referred to the queen, and Sir John Perrot furnished him with strong letters of recommendation to the English court. Thus prepared, he set out for London, in 1587, when his insinuating manners and apparent attachment to the English government so wrought on Elizabeth, that she granted him the earldom and the whole inheritance of Tyrone, with the exception of two hundred and forty acres on the river Blackwater, for the use of a fort which she had ordered to be erected in that quarter: some stipulations were also made in favour of the sons of John and Turlogh O'Neil.

As the new earl of Tyrone was now considered the firmest friend of government in the North, he was authorized to keep six companies constantly on foot to repress any attempt at insurrection. This permission greatly forwarded the design he contemplated, as when he trained them to military evolutions, he dismissed them and levied others in their place, by which means he soon taught the use of arms to all his vassals, and under pretence of roofing a castle which he was building at Dungannon, he imported a considerable quantity of lead; but he took care to reserve it for a very different purpose. He at the same time used every art to extend his influence over the neighbouring Irish lords, and all who opposed his proceedings felt the weight of his power. Maguire and Mac Mahon made loud complaints to the lord deputy of O'Neil's tyrannical conduct, which were transmitted to the queen; but before the government could come to a decision on this point, its attention was directed to the punishment of another powerful malcontent.

Intelligence was received in Dublin that O'Donnel, the chief of Tyrconnel, had refused to admit the queen's sheriff into his district, and that he was carrying on a secret negociation with the Island Scots. This news threw the council into great consternation, as they were now destitute of troops to assert their authority. But Sir John Perrot quieted their apprehensions by assuring them that if they left the affair to his discretion, he would secure the person of either O'Donnel or his son with little expense to her majesty; and this he accomplished by means which tarnished the upright character which he had hitherto sustained, and proved ultimately extremely injurious to the English interests in Ulster. The lord deputy is supposed to have been urged to this dishonorable act by the jealousy which the government entertained of the extraordinary qualifications of Hugh Roe, or Red Hugh O'Donnel, the presumptive heir of Tyrconnel. Though still a youth in his sixteenth year, he had already manifested great independence of character, and a decided aversion to the English dominion: he possessed a vigorous constitution, great courage, and literary talents of no ordinary description; and these qualities, together with the beauty of his person, had rendered him an object of very general admiration throughout Ireland.

About Michaelmas, 1587, the captain of a ship laden with Spanish wines contracted with Sir John Perrot to execute his project of seizing young O'Donnel, and he accordingly sailed for Lough Swilly, where he soon cast anchor off the castle of Dundonald, which was the residence of an Irish lord named Mac Sweeny. The wily captain immediately sent some of his crew to the castle with samples of the wine, which they distributed so freely to the inmates of the fortress that they soon became intoxicated. During this carouse Red Hugh, with some of his young friends, paid a visit to Mac Sweeny, who anxious to display his hospitality to the son of his chief, sent a messenger to the ship to purchase a quantity of the wine. The captain, under some pretext, declined to sell it at that time, but politely invited Mac Sweeny and his guests to an entertainment on board his vessel, which the natural curiosity of Red Hugh and his young associates prompted them to accept. Accompanied by Mac Sweeny, the unsuspecting victims went on board, and being received in the cabin by their treacherous host, with the greatest apparent cordiality, wine and other strong liquors were placed before them: but in the midst of their hilarity their arms were stolen away, and when they awoke from the effects of their excess, they found themselves prisoners. Rejoicing in the success of his stratagem, the captain instantly set sail for Dublin, where he arrived in safety with his captives; and Red Hugh, after a long examination before the council, was sent loaded with irons, to a tower in the castle, where he remained a close prisoner for several years.

This was the last act of Perrot's government, for he soon after solicited and obtained his recal. However dishonorable the seizure of young O'Donnel may appear, it did not alienate from the lord deputy the affections of the natives: before his departure he summoned to court all those Irish lords whom he suspected of favouring a foreign enemy, and prevailed on them to give hostages to government for their loyal intentions; and he presented the mayor and citizens of Dublin with a silver cup gilt, bearing the motto, *In pace relinquo* (I leave you in peace;) and after delivering the sword of state to his successor, Sir William Fitzwilliam, he said, that now, though a private man, he would engage to bring in any suspected leader, within twenty days, without violence or contest. He was accompanied to the water-side by an immense multitude, who bemoaned his departure with loud lamentations; among them old Turlogh Lynogh O'Neil was observed to shed many tears; and a guard of the citizens attended him to his residence at Carew Castle in Pembrokeshire. But Perrot's reception at the court of Elizabeth was very different. He was committed to the Tower, and afterwards found guilty on a variety of charges, none of which were proved, except one, which accused him of uttering disrespectful words of the queen. Elizabeth, however, refused to sign a warrant for the execution of her reputed brother; but he lay in prison till he died about six months after his condemnation.

The year 1588 has become memorable in British history, for the defeat and destruction of the famous Spanish Armada, fitted out by king Philip to enforce the spiritual thunders of Rome against Elizabeth, which declared the throne of the schismatic princess forfeited, and the king of Spain the rightful heir of the house of Lancaster. The high-spirited queen did not wait till this mighty armament should reach her shores, but in 1587 she sent a fleet of thirty sail to the coast of Spain, under that distinguished commander, Sir Francis Drake, who destroyed above one hundred store ships in the harbour of Cadiz, and on his return captured a rich Indian carrack, which amply repaid all the expenses of the expedition. Drake justly boasted that *he had singed king Philip's whiskers;* for his success so crippled the design, that it had to be deferred for another year. Elizabeth employed this interval in the most vigorous preparations to meet the terrible danger which menaced her dominions, and she was nobly seconded by her people. The English

THE SPANISH ARMADA.

navy, at that time, consisted of only *twenty-eight ships*, not one of which exceeded the bulk of a large frigate; but the zeal of the nobility and merchants supplied this deficiency at their own charge, the city of London alone furnishing thirty ships and ten thousand men. The queen gave the command of her fleet to lord Howard of Effingham, having under him Sir Francis Drake, Hawkins, and Frobisher, the most renowned seamen of Europe in that day. As England was then also without a regular army, similar exertions were used to raise land forces; and in an incredibly short space of time more than eighty thousand men were levied, a great part of whom were stationed on the southern coast, while a body of 23,000 formed a camp at Tilbury, to defend the capital; and here the heroic princess frequently appeared on horseback in the midst of her soldiers, to animate them by her presence and eloquence to the defence of their country and religion.

The grand Spanish Armada was ready for sea early in the month of May, and consisted of more than one hundred and fifty vessels, some of very large size, commanded by the duke of Medina Sidonia. It had on board above thirty thousand sailors and soldiers, with two thousand six hundred and thirty pieces of brass cannon; and on arriving off the Flemish coast, the duke of Parma had instructions to join it with all his forces, and then it was expected that England would become an easy conquest. But the Spanish fleet had scarcely set sail from the port of Lisbon, when it was assailed by a furious tempest, which sunk some of the ships and forced the rest to take shelter in the Groyne. After refitting, they again set sail, and in a few days appeared off Plymouth.—When lord Howard with the English fleet got out of port, he soon descried his formidable antagonists advancing towards him in the form of a crescent, which extended to the distance of seven miles from one extremity to the other; but the English admiral adopted the most judicious plan of combat with an enemy so greatly his superior, and after capturing two of their great ships, he kept up a running fight with them till they gained the French coast, and cast anchor before Calais. Lord Howard now sent some fireships among them, by which the Spaniards were so alarmed, that they cut their cables and dispersed, and in the confusion the English captured or destroyed twelve of their ships.

The duke of Medina perceiving that his hopes of success were now at an end, resolved to return homewards; but as the wind opposed his passage through the channel, he was forced to sail northwards, make a tour of Britain, and endeavour to reach his own harbour by the ocean. Want of ammunition prevented the English admiral from following him, and probably compelling the whole armament to surrender. But the elements proved almost equally destructive to this ill-fated expedition, for it was overtaken by a second violent tempest after it had passed the Orkneys, which drove many of the ships on the coast of Scotland and Ireland, where they were miserably wrecked, and it is calculated that scarcely half of the grand Armada returned to Spain.

Seventeen of these unfortunate vessels, containing upwards of five thousand men, were driven on shore in various parts of Ireland.—

One of these called Our Lady of the Rosary, a ship of 1000 tons, foundered off the Blasquets on the coast of Kerry, and in her perished more than six hundred men, amongst whom was the prince of Ascule, Don Pedro, the king of Spain's natural son, and many other persons of distinction. On the coast of Ulster and Connaught, those Spaniards who escaped the fury of the seas were received by the Irish who regarded them as their kinsmen, with the most cordial hospitality; and Hugh O'Neil, earl of Tyrone, while he still avowed his loyalty to the Irish government, was strongly suspected of making secret arrangements with them respecting a future invasion. O'Ruarc of Breffney avowed his attachment to their cause more openly, for when Don Antonio de Leva was cast on his territory with a thousand Spaniards, he not only gave him cordial entertainment, but urged him to remain in the country and declare war against Elizabeth, assuring him that thousands of the Irish would join his standard. De Leva, however, told him that he should first return to Spain, to obtain a commission for the enterprise from his loyal master. But even in sight of the Irish shore the ship foundered, and De Leva with his whole crew perished. — O'Ruarc finding himself abandoned to the vengeance of the government, fled to Scotland, but the influence of Elizabeth was then so powerful at that court, that he was delivered up to the English, and executed in London as a traitor.

Rumours were now circulated, that the Spaniards had left behind them vast treasures in those parts of the country where they had been entertained. This fired the cupidity of the lord deputy, who immediately issued a commission to search out, and secure the property for the queen; but this proving ineffectual, he proceeded to Connaught in June 1589, summoned to his presence all who were charged with giving refuge to the Spaniards, and compelled them to deliver up these unfortunate men, with all the property that belonged to them. Many of these miserable captives were beheaded at Galway by order of Fitzwilliam, who soon after returned to Dublin, without obtaining that treasure which had been the main object of his journey. A similar expedition to Ulster, was attended with no other result than the seizure of Sir Owen O'Toole, father-in-law of the earl of Tyrone, and Sir John O'Dogherty, who were considered as two of the best affected of the Northern leaders. But it was reported that they had possessed themselves of a considerable portion of the Spanish treasure, and this afforded the avaricious viceroy a sufficient pretext for consigning them to prison, where the former lay till he was reduced to the point of death, and the latter, after a rigorous incarceration of two years' continuance, purchased his enlargement with a considerable sum of money.

These arbitrary proceedings of the lord deputy, while they made the loyal Irish apprehensive for their own safety, confirmed the disaffected in their inveterate hatred of the government. The wily Tyrone, however, still found it necessary to dissemble, and trusting to the influence he had gained at the English court, he once more repaired to London, cast himself at the feet of Elizabeth, and renewed his assurance of attachment and fidelity in the most ample form ; agreeing to find securities, and deliver hostages to the lord deputy of Ireland, for his future loyalty and peaceable conduct. He soon, however, found pretexts for eluding the execution of those promises which he had made so liberally before the English council.

About this time Red Hugh O'Donnel contrived to escape from the castle of Dublin, where he had been kept in rigorous confinement for four years. Towards the close of 1591, he and some of his fellow-prisoners, had found means to get off their fetters, and by the aid of a rope, to descend from the top of the tower in which they were immured upon the drawbridge which was then attached to the castle. They escaped, and directing their course to the mountains of Wicklow, reached Fassaroe, (the Red Mountain) before morning. Beyond this poor Red Hugh was unable to proceed, as his old shoes had fallen from his feet, which were terribly bruised by the rough stones and briers of the mountains over which he had travelled during the preceding night. Here his companions were, for their own security, obliged to leave him; but a faithful servant, who had assisted in his escape, was sent to a gentleman in the neighbourhood, named Phelim O'Toole, to claim his protection. O'Toole had been his fellow-prisoner in the castle of Dublin, and before his liberation he and O'Donnel had given mutual pledges to assist each other whenever they had the power; but having now made peace with the government, he forgot all his promises, and instead of affording Red Hugh the aid he required, he seized the unfortunate youth, and sent him back to the lord deputy, by whom he was again loaded with chains, and subjected to a still more rigorous confinement.

But his first failure did not deter Red Hugh from making another effort to escape. By means of a rope which was procured by his faithful servant Turlogh *Buidhe* (or Yellow) O'Hogan, he, and Henry and Arthur, the sons of the late John O'Neil, let themselves down through the funnel of the privy in the wall of the tower, into the Poddle, which river enclosed the castle on that side. They proceeded towards the mountains, with the view of reaching Glen Molawr, the strong hold of

Feagh Mac Hugh O'Byrne, who was then in arms against the government. During the night, which was dark and tempestuous, with heavy drifts of snow, Henry O'Neil was unfortunately separated from his companions, and his brother Arthur, being heavy and corpulent, became at length unable to proceed. Red Hugh, determined not to forsake his friend in this extremity, took shelter with him under a projecting rock, while he sent his servant to Glen Molawr to inform O'Byrne of their situation. The insurgent chief instantly sent some of his followers to their relief with clothes and refreshment: but when they reached the spot, they found them with difficulty, as the snow had completely covered them. Arthur O'Neil was dead, and young O'Donnel so exhausted, that O'Byrne's men had to carry him to the glen, where he remained a considerable time without being able to travel, his feet having been so severely frost-bitten, that he lost the use of his two great toes, which he never afterwards recovered.

When, at length, he was able to ride, Red Hugh and his faithful servant O'Hogan were conveyed across the Liffey by a troop of O'Byrne's horse, although the bridges and fords were strictly guarded by the English. They crossed the Boyne near Drogheda in a fisherman's boat, and passing through Dundalk at full gallop soon reached Dungannon, where they were privately entertained for four days and nights by the earl of Tyrone. His next place of refuge was the house of his half brother Hugh Maguire on the borders of Lough Erne, from whence he ultimately arrived in safety at the castle of Athseanaigh (now Ballyshannon) the princely residence of his father. The escape of Red Hugh was hailed as a triumph by all the clans of the O'Donnels, who on the 3d of May solemnly inaugurated him as their chief, and he soon displayed both talents and inclination to take vengeance for his recent sufferings. The English were expelled from Donegal; Turlogh Lynogh O'Neil was forced to renounce his connexion with them, and a messenger was despatched to the king of Spain, to solicit his aid, while a number of Scotch mercenaries were engaged to assist O'Donnel in the execution of his design.

Red Hugh having about this time married a daughter of the earl of Tyrone, that chief again became suspected, and these suspicions were increased by a variety of other circumstances. He had lately avenged himself on his accuser Hugh Ne Gavelocke by seizing and consigning him to the executioner; and when the state expressed its alarm at this presumptuous act of violence, he pleaded that he had only executed his power of martial law on a notorious traitor. Turlogh O'Neil complained of his outrages, and Sir Henry Bagnal accused him of seducing the affections of his sister, and marrying her while his first wife was living. But this grand dissembler found plausible reasons for all his proceedings, and thus he replied to their several charges, viz.— he had consented to the alliance with O'Donnel to keep him in his allegiance!—the outrages committed on Turlogh O'Neil were the consequence of his own violence; and with regard to Sir Henry Bagnal's accusation, he said, that so far from seducing his sister, she had freely consented to become his wife, and he was at full liberty to accept her, as he had been regularly divorced from his former consort. He, in turn, accused Sir Henry Bagnal, his brother-in-law, with usurping greater authority in Ulster than he was entitled to; but intimated, at the same time that he wished to be reconciled to him, that they might cordially unite their influence in the service of the government. To give a greater air of sincerity to these loyal and peaceful professions, he allowed his territory to be formed into an English county, Dungannon being appointed the shire-town.

I have thus detailed to you the course of dissimulation practised by Hugh earl of Tyrone, while he was consolidating his plans for that rebellion which has had so powerful an influence on our subsequent history, and proved him to be one of the most extraordinary characters both as a negociator and warrior, that our island has ever produced. But a variety of circumstances which occurred in the year 1593 and 1594 compelled him to throw off the cloak of loyalty which he had worn for so many years, and commence that important enterprise that he had been so long meditating.

About the commencement of 1593, a captain Willis was appointed by the lord deputy to be sheriff of Fermanagh, and he proceeded, in the manner too common at that period, to spoil the wretched inhabitants with a numerous and rapacious train of followers, which so provoked Maguire, the chieftain of that territory, that he attacked Willis and his attendants, drove them into a church, and would have put them all to the sword had not Tyrone persuaded him to set them at liberty. This act the earl took care to display advantageously to the English council, and he soon after had a fresh opportunity of exhibiting his pretended loyalty to the government. I say *pretended*, because it is acknowledged even by writers most partial to this singular man, that he kept up all this time a secret correspondence with the insurgent chieftains.

Sir William Fitzwilliam having solicited his dismissal from the Irish government early in 1594, was succeeded by Sir William Russel, a son of the earl of Bedford. The English forces were at this time actively employed against Maguire, who had been declared a traitor. Doctor Magawran, the Roman Catholic prelate of Armagh, resided principally at the house of this chieftain, and having been lately appointed the pope's envoy to the Irish, for the purpose of animating their exertions in the cause of religion, had instigated Maguire to excite some commotions in Connaught, whither this warlike prelate accompanied him. But the expedition proved unfortunate, as Maguire's forces were met on a misty morning at a place called Sciath-na-Feart, by a corps of Sir Richard Bingham's army, commanded by Sir William Guelfort. Owing to the haze the cavalry on both sides unexpectedly met front to front, when Maguire instantly transfixed Guelfort with a spear, and slew him on the spot. Nearly at the same moment some British horsemen rushing on the archbishop and his attendants, the prelate shared a similar fate with that of the English commander, and Maguire deemed it prudent to retire within his own territory.

Sir Henry Bagnal being now ordered to pursue Maguire into Fermanagh, the earl of Tyrone attended his standard with all the alacrity of a faithful subject, and distinguished himself with such zeal, that in one of the subsequent actions he received a wound in the thigh; but he soon after withdrew from the camp, and took no further part in these hostilities. Maguire having been defeated near Lough Erne, Bagnal got possession of the castle of Enniskillen, in which he placed a strong garrison; but no sooner had the English army retired than young O'Donnel invested the fortress, and continued the siege from June to August, when he was suddenly called off by the arrival of his Scotch auxiliaries in Lough Foyle. During his absence the English again advanced to relieve the castle, but they met such a decisive defeat, that they were compelled to abandon all their baggage and provisions, among which there was such a quantity of biscuits, that the scene of action was from this circumstance denominated the *Ford of Biscuits*. The garrison of the castle surrendered soon after, and were butchered without mercy, the conquerors pleading as their excuse that the English captors had set them the example by treating the Irish garrison of the fort in the same manner.

These successes encouraged the enterprising O'Donnel to make frequent inroads into Connaught in the following spring, during which he razed several castles, and committed terrible depredations on the English settlers; and eluding every attempt of Sir Richard Bingham to intercept him, returned to his own country with a great booty of cattle and treasure. In these excursions he found most efficient support from six hundred Scottish auxiliaries under Mac Leod of Arra.

The English government now becoming justly alarmed at these violent proceedings, determined on sending three thousand additional troops to Ireland, under the command of Sir John Norris, a highly distinguished leader. It was also declared that a chain of forts should be formed round the territory of the disaffected lords of Ulster, so as to keep them in awe, and effectually restrain their predatory expeditions. Tyrone had hitherto waited for foreign aid before he came to an open rupture with the government, but he now conceived it necessary to throw off the mask, lest the hopes of the disaffected should be completely crushed by the projected measures. He accordingly entered into an alliance, early in 1595, with the various branches of the O'Neils, O'Donnels, Maguires, Magenisses, Mac Donnels, and O'Cahans, and was appointed commander-in-chief of their united forces. Emboldened by this union, Tyrone, though now in his 58th year, commenced hostilities with all the vigour of youth. He attacked and stormed the fort of Portmor built on the verge of the Blackwater, and after razing it to the ground, proceeded, with the aid of Mac Mahon and Maguire, to lay siege to the castle of Monaghan. He at the same time sent fresh emissaries to Spain, requiring assistance, and sought, though in vain, to detach the earl of Kildare from his allegiance.

While engaged in these treasonable proceedings, he despatched letters to the lord deputy professing the most loyal attachment to the crown. But Bagnal, his vigilant enemy, intercepted those letters, and having advanced from Newry to the relief of Monaghan at the head of eighteen hundred men, forced his way, after a conflict of three hours, through a narrow pass which was defended by Tyrone in person, and compelled the insurgents to raise the siege of the castle of Monaghan. He then reinforced and revictualled the fortress; but on his return to Newry he was suddenly attacked by nine thousand of Tyrone's troops, yet he effected his retreat with the loss of twenty killed and nineteen wounded, while three hundred of the Irish are said to have fallen in the conflict.

A considerable force having been collected at Dundalk, Russel, the lord deputy, accompanied by Sir John Norris, advanced against the insurgents on the 24th of June, O'Molloy and O'Hanlon, two Irish chieftains, alternately bearing the viceroy's standard. The English marched through Armagh, in which they placed a strong garrison, and reached Monaghan on the 3d of July. Tyrone, after having set fire to Dungannon, retired before the royal army to his inaccessible haunts, and the viceroy in a few days returned to Dublin. But he had scarcely retired when Tyrone and O'Donnel again invested the castle: Sir John Norris advanced a second time to its relief, and an action ensued which was distinguished by some feats of valour which have been rarely surpassed. The English endeavoured to force the pass of Cluain-Tibhin, which was surrounded by deep morasses, and bravely defended by the Irish. In this gallant attempt the English general had his horse shot under him, and both he and his brother were wounded. Sedgrave, a native of Meath, an officer of great bodily strength and distinguished heroism, now rushed impetuously forward at the head of a troop of cavalry, and made good his passage across the ford. Tyrone met him in mid career, and the spears of the two champions were shivered on their armour. But Sedgrave, with desperate valour, seized the earl by the neck and dragged him from his horse, while Tyrone, at the same time, firmly grasping his adversary, the warriors fell struggling to the earth. The earl being undermost, his fate was considered decided, but he fortunately found means to thrust his dagger into Sedgrave's groin, under his armour, which killed him in a moment, and the English retired in dismay from the conflict.

The government alarmed at the boldness and success of the insurgent chiefs, had now the weakness to propose a negociation with them; and commissioners were appointed to hear their complaints, and receive from them any overtures that might lead to an accommodation. As Tyrone and O'Donnel refused to risque their persons in any walled town, the parties met in an open field, where the former complained of the injustice with which Bagnal had treated him, in encroaching upon his just rights, and his implacable resentment in attempting to separate him from his wife, who had now sunk under his cruelty. He demanded a free pardon for himself and his followers, with the full exercise of their religion—that his country should be freed from English garrisons and sheriffs, and that all who had ravaged his territory should be compelled to make restitution.— O'Donnel complained of his long imprisonment and other injuries, while each inferior chieftain had his grievances to urge. The commissioners acknowledged some of their allegations to be just, but on the material points no decision could be made until the queen's pleasure should be known. In the mean time, the commissioners demanded that the insurgents should lay down their arms, admit sheriffs into their territories, repair the forts they had demolished, and discover upon oath their transactions with foreign princes. But the Irish lords rejected these terms with disdain, and the conference broke up, after agreeing to a suspension of hostilities till the 1st of January, 1596.

Soon after the expiration of the truce, Tyrone made a grand effort to regain Armagh, and with that object he attacked a considerable force of Norris's army, which was stationed at the church of Killoter. They were forced to give way to the desperate valour of the Irish, and after losing many of their number, they fled through Armagh to Dundalk, having left a garrison of five hundred men under captain Stafford for the defence of the former place. Tyrone being now master of the surrounding country, took the most effectual means to cut off all communication between Armagh and the English army, by which the garrison soon became a prey to famine and disease. Sir John Norris made an attempt to relieve the city by forwarding a quantity of provisions from Dundalk, under an escort of a squadron of horse and three companies of foot: but through the vigilance of Tyrone the escort was defeated and captured with the whole convoy, and the chieftain stripping the British soldiers, equipped an equal number of his own men in their uniforms. He placed one half of these under Con O'Neil, in the vaults of a ruined monastery which was situated eastward of the city; and with the remainder he appeared at dawn of day in full view of the garrison. A sham fight soon commenced between those who were dressed in the English uniform and another body of the Irish army, the men on each side firing their muskets which were charged only with powder, and many of the soldiers fell to the ground as if struck by the shot of their antagonists. Completely deceived by this stratagem, Stafford sent forth half his garrison to the assistance of his supposed countrymen; but when the English advanced to the conflict, they suddenly found themselves assailed by the troops whom they had been so eager to succour, as well as by Tyrone's forces; and in the midst of their confusion Con O'Neil sprang forth with his corps from the old monastery, and the whole party thus attacked in front and rear were put to the sword in the very view of the garrison. Stafford was so weakened by this disaster, that he surrendered the city on being permitted to retire to Dundalk.

The success of the northern insurgents now fanned the flame of rebellion in all the other provinces. The disaffected in Munster began to display a turbulent disposition, and the Irish chieftains of Leinster extended their outrages from Wexford to the very gates of the capital. But, next to Ulster, Connaught, through the never-ceasing activity of Red Hugh O'Donnel, was now the principal seat of insurrection. In the month of May, he received in great state, at Lifford, Don Alonzo Copis, an emissary from the king of Spain, by whom he wrote letters to that monarch, intreating speedy succours of men, arms, and stores to deliver them from the yoke of the English oppressor. Hearing, soon after, that Sir John Norris, aided by the earls of Thomond and Clanrickard, was assembling a powerful force on the frontiers of Connaught, he suddenly marched his troops into that province, and being joined by many of the chieftains with their forces, he encamped in the neighbourhood of the royal army, which soon found it prudent to retreat.

The English general now marched with the lord deputy into Ulster, with a force so powerful, that Tyrone was obliged to abandon his conquests, and retire to his fastnesses, whither the devastated state of the country did not permit the viceroy to pursue him; and after placing fresh garrisons in Armagh and Monaghan, and condemning Tyrone and his principal associates as traitors, he left Sir John Norris on the borders to watch the motions of the rebels. Want of provisions and the approach of winter, as well as the non-appearance of succours from Spain, induced Tyrone once more to resort to his old arts of dissimulation, and he sent letters of penitence, and submission both to the queen and Sir John Norris. The English general had long wished to act with moderation towards the insurgent lords, and the queen was anxious to settle the affairs of Ireland on any reasonable terms. She now granted a commission to Sir John Norris and Sir Geoffry Fenton, her Irish Secretary of State, to grant pardon to all rebels who should, with due humility, seek her royal mercy: Tyrone, O'Donnel, Maguire, and many others of their confederates, accordingly appeared at Dundalk, and submitted to the terms which they had formerly rejected, and a promise of pardon was delivered to each lord.

The northern war appearing now at an end, Sir William Russel and Norris marched into Connaught to suppress the commotions of that province. The mal-contents retired before the royal forces, and every castle surrendered on the first summons, except that of Losmage belonging to O'Madden, who valorously replied, that he would not surrender, though the whole English army were lord deputies. But this foolish boast was punished by storming the castle, and putting the whole garrison to the sword. Such loud complaints were made by the chieftains who submitted, of the tyrannical conduct of Sir Richard Bingham, the president, that indignant at those charges, he repaired to England without licence, to justify himself before the queen. He was, however, committed to prison, and Sir Conyers Clifford appointed to succeed him: yet he afterwards so completely disproved the accusations that were brought against him, that he was restored to favour, and employed by the government.

While the disaffected lords of Connaught were thus reserving their strength for a more favourable opportunity, the arrival of a few vessels from Spain on the northern coast with a supply of ammunition and some encouraging letters from the king, rendered Tyrone and his associates ashamed of their late concessions, and they found various pretexts for evading the treaty. But they still continued to amuse the government with professions of the most dutiful loyalty, while they were rousing by their emissaries the other provinces to action, and training to arms the conflux of men which poured into their territories from every quarter of the kingdom. In these proceedings they were encouraged by the evident weakness of the government in proposing another conference, at which Meyler Magrath archbishop of Cashel, and Thomas earl of Ormond, were appointed to act as the queen's commissioners. But Tyrone and his confederates, as on a former occasion, refused to attend the commissioners in a walled town, and thus the project terminated.

The imperious Elizabeth now became terribly provoked at the continuance of this harassing war; and through the instigation of the earl of Essex, she was led to cast much of the blame of its ill success on the brave Sir John Norris, of whom her favorite was the avowed enemy and rival. He was in consequence abruptly dismissed to his government of Munster, where his noble spirit sunk under the disgrace in two months, when he expired in the arms of his brother. Sir William Russel being recalled about the same time, the whole authority of the state both civil and military was committed to Thomas lord Borough, a nobleman esteemed as possessing considerable vigour and talents for war.

This viceroy entered on his government with the determination of an active prosecution of the rebels. He accordingly marched into Ulster in June 1597 with a considerable army, Henry earl of Kildare, and other lords of the Pale attending his standard with their followers; while Sir Conyers Clifford was ordered to march from Connaught with seventeen hundred men, and meet him at the Black-water. Tyrone, apprised of these intended movements, detached five hundred men into Leinster to excite his friends in that quarter to intercept Clifford on his march. The command of this body was entrusted to an officer named Tirrel, who, though of English origin, was a zealous Roman Catholic, and firmly attached to the Irish.—Sir Conyers Clifford, having entered Westmeath, detached young Barnwell, a son of lord Trimbleston, against him, at the head of a thousand men from Mullingar; but the Irish commander aware of their approach, appeared to fly before them, and having gained a defile concealed with trees, (since called Tirrel's

Pass) he detached half of his little army, under lieutenant O'Connor, a skilful and gallant soldier, who posted his men in ambuscade in a hollow ground near the road over which the English troops were to march. Barnwell, eager in the pursuit, had scarcely passed his concealed enemies, when O'Connor rushed out on his rear with a tremendous noise of drums and bagpipes, which was the signal agreed upon by Tirrel, who immediately returned to the conflict; and the English, thus placed between two fires, are said to have been entirely cut off, with the exception of their commander who was taken prisoner, and one private soldier who escaped through a marsh. Our Irish historians tell us that O'Connor exhibited great personal prowess in this action, and that his hand was so swollen with incessant muscular action, that it could not be removed from the guard of his sabre until the steel was separated with a file! Sir Conyers Clifford was now compelled to retreat with the scanty remnant of his forces, but this movement he effected with consummate skill in the presence of an army three times his number.

In the mean time the enterprising O'Donnel had created a powerful diversion in Connaught. Having collected his forces early in spring, he laid siege to Athenry, which he took by escalade, and then set fire to the town, after having first secured a great booty of arms, clothing and ammunition. He afterwards marched towards Galway, devastating the whole country in his route. But he met such a determined resistance that he was compelled to retire, having first set fire to the eastern suburbs of the town. He had many actions with the royal forces in Connaught during this summer, in one of which Murrogh O'Brien, lord Inchiquin, was killed by a musket ball.

But the defeat of Clifford and the untoward events in Connaught did not deter the lord deputy from marching into Ulster, which was now with the exception of some strong castles entirely in the hands of the rebels. On approaching Armagh he found Tyrone's army strongly intrenched in a narrow pass, but lord Borough attacked him with such vigour, that the Irish chieftain, after a brave resistance, was driven from his position, and the lord deputy now marching through Armagh, carried the strong fort of Portmor on the river Blackwater by assault. During these events Tyrone's troops lay concealed in the adjoining woods, and while lord Borough and his army were engaged in returning thanks to God for their recent success, the Irish were perceived descending a neighbouring hill in considerable force. Henry earl of Kildare was detached against them with a division of the royal army. He attacked and repulsed them with the greatest bravery; but two of his foster brothers being slain while rescuing him from the hands of the enemy, this brave and generous young nobleman was so afflicted by the event, that he died a few days after lamenting their premature death. Nor did the lord deputy long survive him, for being suddenly taken ill, he returned towards Dublin, and expired before he reached the capital.

Such are the circumstances attending the fall of these illustrious men as related by the English writers, from which the accounts of our Irish historians materially differ. They tell us that after lord Borough had crossed the Blackwater, his further progress was checked by a body of Irish troops under Cormac and Art O'Neil, which were posted on the left bank of the river, on the road to Benburb, while Tyrone himself with James M'Donnel of the Glinnes, occupied the position of Tibhir-Masain: that the deputy in attempting to force his way through these two corps, was mortally wounded—that Kildare, on whom the command of the royal forces devolved, with his foster-brothers, met with a similar fate, and that the English were completely routed. Whatever may have been the true state of the case, it is clear that Tyrone retained all the advantages which he possessed at the opening of the campaign, with the exception of the fort on the Blackwater.

Loftus, archbishop of Dublin, and Sir Robert Gardiner, the chief justice, were now appointed lords justices, while the command of the army was entrusted to the earl of Ormond. The state of Leinster had become, by this time, so alarming, that Ormond could not quit that province; Sir Henry Bagnal was, therefore, commissioned to watch the movements of the northern insurgents. The wily Tyrone resorted once more to his old artifice, and solicited a suspension of hostilities. He affected extraordinary satisfaction at the high authority committed to the earl of Ormond, from whom he expected the regards of a countryman, and implored his interposition with the queen in favour of a repentant offender, whose foul relapses could not indeed be justified, but were palliated by the numerous wrongs which he had sustained. The earl of Ormond having procured a commission to treat with him, a cessation of arms was agreed upon for two months; and after a tedious negociation, the necessity or weakness of the English government caused them to grant him a free pardon on his own terms. But learning soon after that speedy assistance might be expected from Spain, he once more, under various pretexts, eluded the fulfilment of his promises, and instead of pleading his pardon, he re-commenced hostilities in the summer of 1598, and in conjunction with O'Donnel attempted to carry the fort of Portmor by escalade. But the brave garrison precipitated the first assailants headlong from the ramparts, and exhibited such a determination to resist to the uttermost, that Tyrone was forced to change the siege into a blockade. He occupied all the avenues by which provisions could be thrown either into that place or Armagh; yet the besieged, animated by the heroic example and exhortations of Williams, their governor, refused to yield, though they were at length compelled to live on the flesh of their horses, and the wild herbs that grew in the ditches that surrounded the fort.

Field-marshal Bagnal was now ordered to march with a considerable force to the relief of Portmor and Armagh; and the desertion of Con O'Neil, Tyrone's illegitimate son, to the English, favoured the design. Through his guidance Armagh was victualled by a large division of Bagnal's troops, who marched by an unfrequented road; and, encouraged by this success, the English proceeded, in the following night, accompanied by the deserter, to Tyrone's encampment, where they surprised and slew the earl's advanced guard, and the great chieftain himself was not apprised of his danger till they burst into his tent, from whence he escaped in his shirt. But before day-break he re-assembled his troops, order was restored in the camp, and his adversaries retired.

Bagnal's army was now strongly reinforced, and he was ordered to relieve the fort of Portmor at every risk. He accordingly proceeded, in the month of August, towards the Blackwater, at the head of four thousand five hundred foot, and four hundred horse. Nor was Tyrone unprepared to meet the man whom he considered his deadly foe, the junction of his associates O'Donnel, Maguire, and Mac William Bourke, having increased his forces to more than five thousand men, while no means were neglected to inspire the Irish army with an enthusiastic determination to defend what they were taught to consider the cause of their country.

As this battle proved one of the most important that had taken place since the English invasion, and displayed more military skill than usual on both sides, I shall be somewhat particular in its description. On the 10th of August the royal army marched from Armagh before sunrise, with the sound of martial music, the wings being formed of musketeers and cavalry, and the centre of spearmen, disposed in three corps. They passed unmolested till about seven o'clock, when they entered a narrow pass which contained some trees and thickets, where Tyrone had posted five hundred light armed infantry, who kept up a well-directed fire on the English, by which many of them perished. But Bagnal forced his way through the pass with great gallantry, and reached an extensive plain, on which the Irish camp was situated. At the extremity of this plain Tyrone had dug pit-falls and trenches, which were covered with a network of wattles, and the surface carefully strewed with herbage. Into these many of the English cuirassiers, while rushing forward, unconscious of danger, were precipitated, and dreadfully maimed; and scarcely had they reformed their ranks, when they were assailed by a host of Tyrone's light troops, who were armed with pikes ten or twelve feet in length, for which the shorter spears of the English cavalry were by no means a match. Yet the gallant Bagnal fought his way through all these difficulties till he came within a short distance of the Irish camp, where new obstacles presented themselves. Here the plain was skirted on one side by a marsh, on the other by a moor and a wood, which thus narrowed it to a strait. Across this strait Tyrone had thrown up a rampart four feet high, and sunk a fosse of considerable depth. Water from the marshes flowed in the front, and hence the place was called *Beal na ath Buidhe*, ' the Mouth of the Yellow Ford.'

To surmount this obstruction, the English commander made the most desperate efforts; but in the very tempest of the fight, a quantity of gunpowder accidentally took fire, which blew many of his bravest men to atoms. Yet notwithstanding this disaster, he succeeded, by a heavy cannonade, in levelling a part of the rampart, through which two strong divisions burst into the level ground, and attacked the right and left wings of the Irish under Tyrone and O'Donnel. Bagnal advanced to support them at the head of the reserve; but at the moment when he considered the victory his own, he unfortunately raised his beaver, that he might have a better view of the fight, and a musket-ball entering his forehead, he fell dead to the earth. This terrible event threw his division into immediate confusion, and though the other corps continued the conflict with the greatest bravery, the English army was ultimately routed, with the loss of thirteen superior officers, and above fifteen hundred soldiers, all their artillery, ammunition, and provisions, thirty-four stand of colours, and the military chest, containing twelve thousand pieces of gold. Tyrone acknowledged the loss of his army to have amounted to eight hundred killed and wounded.

O'Reilly, a gallant Irish auxiliary of the English, lost his life in endeavouring to cover the retreat of the remnant of the royal troops, who were at length conducted to Armagh by the bravery and address of Montague, the commander of the cavalry; but they were forced to abandon it in the night by Terence O'Hanlon, at the head of the Irish horse, and the city, with the fort of Portmor, immediately surrendered to the victorious Tyrone.

CHAPTER XII.

Effects of Tyrone's Victory—Insurgents in Leinster and Munster—Rory O'Moore—The Sugan Earl of Desmond—Robert Earl of Essex Lord Lieutenant—Action at the Pass of Plumes—Defeat of the Royal Forces by O'Byrne of Wicklow—Vigorous Hostilities of Red Hugh O'Donnel—Battle at the Curlew Mountains—Death of Sir Conyers Clifford—Conference near Dundalk between Essex and Tyrone—Discontent of the Queen and the English Council—Fall of Essex—Tyrone's Manifesto—His visit to Munster—Death of Sir Thomas Norris and Sir Warham St. Leger—Charles Lord Mountjoy Lord Lieutenant—Sir George Carew President of Munster—Vigor of the new Viceroy—Tyrone escapes into Ulster—Capture of the Earl of Ormond by Rory O'More—Sir Henry Dockwra captures Derry—Action at the Moyry Pass—Insurrection in Leinster—Death of O'More—Affairs of Munster—

Florence Mac Arthy—Action near Kinsale—The President's March to Limerick—Surrender of the Castle of Lough-Gur—Attempt of Dermod O'Connor to seize the Earl of Desmond—Siege of Glin Castle—Exploits of Maurice Stack—Capture of the Castle of Lixnaw—Murder of Maurice Stack—The Titular Earl a Fugitive—Lord James Fitzgerald restored to the Earldom of Desmond—His reception at Kilmallock—Death of Dermod O'Connor—Sir Charles Wilmot—Siege of Listowel—Singular preservation of Lord Kerry's Son—Submission of the Munster Rebels—Seizure of the Titular Earl.

THE decisive victory gained by the earl of Tyrone caused the flame of insurrection to spread from province to province, and the illustrious O'Neil was every where hailed as the deliverer of his country. All the chiefs of Ulster and Connaught declared for him; and the Irish septs of Leinster now renewed their outrages in full fury, and bade defiance to the English government. Rory O'More, after regaining possession of the Queen's County, (Leix,) his ancient patrimony, burst into Munster at the head of four thousand men, and was speedily joined by the lords Kerry, Mountgarret, Fermoy, Cahir, the Knight of the Valley, the White Knight, with all the Geraldines and others who had forfeited their lands by Desmond's rebellion; and as the only son of that unfortunate lord was now in the hands of the queen, his nephew James was invested by the mal-contents with all the titles and estates of his family, and he was designated by the English, through the whole of the subsequent insurrection in the south, the *Sugan* earl, (that is, *earl of straw*,) or pretending earl of Desmond. These honors and privileges he stipulated to hold of THE O'NEIL, as Tyrone, having assumed his ancient title, was now emphatically called. There was at this time no force in Munster to resist the progress of the rebels, Sir Walter Raleigh and the other great undertakers having sold or abandoned the lands which had been granted to them: Sir Thomas Norris, the president, was consequently forced to shut himself up in Cork, and the whole province became a wide theatre of crime and devastation. Of the few English settlers that remained, the men were butchered without mercy, and the women subjected to the brutal violence of undisciplined troops, infuriated at once by religious zeal and political animosity.

The fearful progress of the rebellion in Ireland now raised just apprehensions in the English government for the security of their authority in the country. For five years Tyrone had maintained his ground against their ablest generals and bravest troops, and his recent unexpected success had thrown the whole kingdom into a ferment. Intelligence was also received that the king of Spain was preparing a fresh invasion of England, with forty thousand men, while twelve thousand of his troops were destined for the assistance of the insurgent Irish. It was, therefore, resolved to use no longer temporizing expedients, but to send a formidable army, under an experienced general, into Ireland, and thus at once to crush the hopes both of their foreign and domestic enemies. Twenty thousand men were allotted for this service ; the choice of a commander was, however, for some time debated in the council. The queen recommended Sir Charles Blount, lord Mountjoy, for the important office; but this was warmly opposed by her prime favorite, and Mountjoy's personal rival, Robert, earl of Essex, who argued that the retired and studious habits of that nobleman were ill calculated for a course of vigour and activity. It soon appeared that the aspiring favorite, who had already displayed his military talents in Spain and America, sought the dangerous post of pre-eminence for himself; and both his friends and enemies had different motives for gratifying his wish. He was appointed lord lieutenant of Ireland, with authority, civil and military, beyond that of most of his predecessors; and he landed at Dublin, in all the pomp of a military hero, on the 15th of April, 1599.

The insurgents, far from being intimidated at these preparations for their overthrow, made use of them as a stimulus to inspire their countrymen with fresh resolution in defence of their rights and liberties. Nor did the commencement of the new viceroy's administration suggest any fears that they had much to dread from his exertions. Instead of marching in full force to the North, as he had been directed, and inflicting a severe blow on the insurgents in that grand focus of the rebellion, he proceeded towards Munster, at the instigation of some of his privy counsellors, who were deeply interested in the newly planted lands of that province. In passing through Leinster, the vigilant O'More fell upon his rear, killed several of his officers and men, and took from his gay soldiers such a quantity of feathers, that the Irish facetiously called the scene of the action, THE PASS OF PLUMES. After spending ten days in the siege, he captured the castle of Cahir, and then marched through Munster without opposition, the rebels retiring every where at his approach.

While Essex was thus making a useless display of his force in a country where no enemy would meet him, Tyrone was making active preparations for a vigorous campaign. Having obtained a supply of ammunition from Spain, and received some Scottish mercenaries into his service, he assembled an army of more than ten thousand men, part of whom he posted at the passes of Lough Foyle and Ballyshannon, and placed the remainder in an intrenched camp between Newry and Dundalk. The English government now began to express great dissatisfaction at the conduct of the viceroy, which was augmented by intelligence of the shameful defeat of six hundred of the royal forces by O'Byrne of Wicklow. Essex vented his rage on the unfortunate survivors by executing an Irish lieutenant, cashiering the officers, and putting every tenth soldier to death. He now received a sharp rebuke from the queen for his southern expedition, with peremptory orders to proceed to Ulster. He requested a reinforcement of two thousand men, which being granted to him, he commenced his march for the northern province.

He had previously issued orders to Sir Conyers Clifford, the lord president of Connaught, to march towards Beleek, with all the forces he could collect, and make a diversion on that side. But Clifford found an insuperable obstacle to all his plans in the unremitting vigilance of Red Hugh O'Donnel, who after having spent the spring of this year in ravaging Thomond, was now besieging O'Connor Sligo, in the castle of Culmine. Clifford was ordered to make every possible effort to relieve the castle by land, while Theobald ny Lung Bourke, son of the celebrated Grace O'Maley, proceeded with a squadron of ships from Galway, carrying military stores for the use of the besieged. When O'Donnel heard of these preparations, he left the conduct of the siege to his kinsman Neil Garbh O'Donnel, while with the remainder of his army, he took post in the Curlew mountains, and here he continued for two months watching his destined prey. The march of the English was at length announced, and as a battle was inevitable, O'Donnel, on the preceding evening, addressed an inspiriting harangue to his troops, in which he advised them, as the best preparation for death, to go to confession, and in the morning to receive the sacrament. Their devotions had scarcely ended when the English, amounting to seventeen hundred men, appeared in sight, and their advanced guard had but just entered the mountains when O'Rourke, a distinguished Irish leader, sprung from an ambush at the head of two hundred men, and attacked them with such fury, that one hundred and twenty fell at the first onset, amongst whom was the gallant and humane Sir Conyers Clifford. Intimidated by the loss of their leader, the royal forces instantly abandoned the field; the castle of Culmine soon after submitted, and the terror of Red Hugh O'Donnel extended from Sligo to Loop's head.

The loss in this action was trifling, but the moral influence which it had on the English soldiers and their Irish auxiliaries was incalculable, and the desertions became so numerous, that when Essex arrived on the borders of Ulster, he could not muster four thousand men. Yet inferior as his forces were to Tyrone's army, the Irish chieftain was unwilling again to try the fate of battle, till the arrival of the powerful succours which he had been promised by Spain. He had, therefore, recourse to his old artifices for protracting the war, and prevailed on the lord lieutenant to grant him a conference, assuring his lordship that he was ready to cast himself on the queen's mercy. A ford, in the neigbourhood of Dundalk, was the place appointed for the parley, and when Essex appeared on the bank of the river, with all the dignity of a superior, Tyrone plunged into the stream, up to his horse's saddle, as if anxious to throw himself at the feet of the viceroy. They maintained a private conversation for some time, in which the romantic Essex is said to have given some hints of his ill-digested schemes of ambition, while the Irish chief assured him that if he would be guided by his counsel, he would make him the greatest lord in England. Lord Southampton, and some other officers, now joined the viceroy, and Tyrone was attended by his brother Cormac and a few Irish chiefs, when a conference was opened in due form, at which the earl proposed, for himself and his friends, that they would return to their allegiance on the conditions of a general amnesty, the restoration of their lands, the free exercise of their religion, and the exemption of their territories from English jurisdiction. Essex promised to transmit their desires to the queen, which he was accused of having admitted to be just and reasonable, and the parties separated after agreeing to a truce for six weeks.

Elizabeth and her council, when made acquainted with the particulars of this conference, were filled with indignation; but as the queen was apprehensive of some clandestine scheme of ambition on the part of Essex, she feared to provoke his impetuous temper by suddenly recalling him from the Irish government. She, therefore, contented herself for the present with addressing a letter to him and his council, in which she enlarged on the misconduct of the war, in terms that cut the viceroy to the heart. He burst into extravagant menaces of vengeance against his enemies, and even threatened to cross over to England, with the flower of his army, and punish their temerity. But the advice of his friends moderated these furious ebullitions; and he contented himself with placing the government in the hands of Archbishop Loftus and Sir George Carew, and repairing privately to London, to vindicate his conduct to his royal mistress. It soon, however, appeared that he trusted too sanguinely to his former influence with Elizabeth, and in a few months the career of the rash and unfortunate Essex was closed on the scaffold.

All these events only tended to confirm the disaffected Irish lords in their pursuit of what they considered the path of honour; and Tyrone now received additional encouragement by the arrival of a large supply of money and ammunition from Spain, with assurances of a speedy and powerful reinforcement of troops from that country. At the same time arrived Don Matthew Oviedo, a Spanish ecclesiastic, whom the pope had nominated archbishop of Dublin, and by whom the Holy Father sent a present to the prince of Ulster (as Tyrone was now called) of a hallowed plume, which he gravely declared to be the *feathers of a phœnix.*

Tyrone was so elevated by these new honors and promises, that he recommenced hostilities as soon as the truce had expired. He published a manifesto to all his countrymen, exhorting them to forsake the shameful course of heresy, and to unite with him in arms to defend the liberty of their country, and especially of the Catholic religion, which was so dear to him that he was willing to sacrifice every personal feeling rather than abandon its sacred interests. Having prevailed on the earl of Ormond, who again commanded the royal forces, to renew the truce for a month, he, under pretence of a pilgrimage to the abbey of Holy Cross, in Tipperary, entered Munster with two thousand five hundred men, but his real design was to animate his southern associates with fresh ardour in the cause to which he was devoted, and during his stay in that province he exercised all the rights of a sovereign prince. The lands of all who opposed him were ravaged without mercy. He deposed Mac Arthy earl of Clancare, and elevated Florence Mac Arthy, one of his most subtle partisans, to the dignity of Mac Arthy More. At his instigation the titular earl of Desmond forwarded a letter to the king of Spain, in which, after a magnificent display of his services, he required his majesty's aid for the subjugation of his remaining enemies.—Another letter addressed to the pope by Tyrone, Desmond, and Mac Arthy More, required the renewal of the sentence of excommunication against queen Elizabeth, but the pope did not think it prudent at this time to comply with their request; he, however, granted to prince O'Neil and his confederates the same indulgences which had been conferred on those who fought against the Saracens for the recovery of the Holy Land.

All Munster was now in possession of the rebels, with the exception of the fortified towns, in which the royalists had shut themselves up. To add to the dismay of the well-affected, Sir Thomas Norris, the lord president, died at Mallow, of a wound he received in a skirmish with the Bourkes, while Sir Warham St. Leger, the governor of Cork, was slain near that city by the northern chieftain Maguire, but not till after he had inflicted on his antagonist a mortal wound. Ormond, unable to repress these disorders, made an alarming representation of the state of the country to the English government, in consequence of which Sir Charles Blount, lord Mountjoy, was appointed chief governor, and Sir George Carew, lord president of Munster. The new viceroy, having been a younger son of an ancient and honourable family, was originally bred to the law; but visiting the court of Elizabeth through curiosity, when scarcely arrived at his twentieth year, his person and manners attracted the queen's attention; he received sufficient encouragement to commence courtier, and was soon after rewarded with the honor of knighthood. His exertions in the defeat of the Spanish Armada tended to forward his interest at court. He afterwards learnt the art of war in Britanny, under Sir John Norris; and in 1594, by the death of his elder brother, he succeeded to a title, which the prodigality of his father had scarcely left any patrimony to maintain.

Mountjoy was a man of studious habits and refined manners, well acquainted with theology, history, mathematics, and natural philosophy; but as he had hitherto given no proofs of great military genius, those who were unacquainted with the treasures of his mind or the versatility of his talents, viewed him as a mere scholar, unfit for active exertion in the field. Tyrone is stated to have entertained so mean an opinion of the new viceroy, that he exultingly exclaimed, " he would lose the season of action while his breakfast was preparing." The queen herself appears to have employed him with great diffidence, and to have placed her chief hopes on the earl of Ormond, who still retained the command of the army, and Sir George Carew the new president of Munster.

But the vigorous conduct of lord Mountjoy soon displayed the fallacy of these anticipations. He resolved strictly to follow his instructions to encompass the northern insurgents, and cut off their supplies; and having received intelligence the day after his arrival, that Tyrone was in the west of Munster with a considerable force, and that the earls of Ormond, Thomond, and Clanrickard, had so hemmed him in that he could not possibly escape, except by the western borders of the Pale, he marched immediately to Mullingar, to intercept his retreat in that direction. But he soon received the mortifying intelligence that Tyrone had contrived to cross the river Inny, and passed precipitately into the North. This event excited the viceroy's suspicions of those lords who were appointed to watch the movements of the

SEIZURE OF THE EARL OF ORMOND.

great northern insurgent, and these feelings received additional strength from the following incident.

Sir George Carew, accompanied by the earl of Thomond, lord Audley, and eight hundred horse and foot, proceeded early in the month of April, to take upon him his office of president of Munster. At the castle of Kilkenny he was magnificently received by the earl of Ormond, who informed him that he had agreed on the following morning to hold a parley with O'More, the great Leinster insurgent, and invited him and the earl of Thomond to attend the conference. The president, apprehensive for the consequences, offered to collect his hundred cavalry who were cantoned in the surrounding country, but the earl said there was no need of them, and went to the place of meeting with only seventeen horsemen, and a few lawyers and citizens armed with swords, two hundred infantry being posted about two miles in his rear. The place appointed for the conference was a heath called Coronneduff, eight miles from Kilkenny, and here they found O'More with a choice troop of horse, while five hundred of his foot were in view in a wood, within half cannon shot. After Ormond and the rebel chieftain had continued conversing for more than an hour without coming to any agreement, Sir George Carew manifested considerable uneasiness, and warned the earl to retire; but Ormond expressed a wish to speak with Archer, a celebrated jesuit, who attended O'More, and a violent altercation commenced between them, during which, the royal party became gradually surrounded by the insurgents from the wood. Carew and Thomond now put spurs to their horses, and burst through the enemy, but not without injury, the latter having received a pike-wound in his back. Ormond was unhorsed and taken prisoner, nor could the president's exertions arouse his followers to attempt his rescue. He, therefore, after leaving in Kilkenny five hundred men for the protection of the countess and her family, continued his route to Waterford.

The spirits of the insurgents were every where elated by the seizure of Ormond, and strong suspicions were excited among the royalists, that the earl had willingly surrendered himself to O'More, and that his followers being now deprived of their head, would unite with the opponents of government. O'More demanded terms for the liberation of his noble captive, which were rejected with disdain by Mountjoy, who was determined, though the whole military force in Ireland did not, at that time, exceed fifteen thousand men, that this disaster should not cause him to relax in his exertions against the northern rebels. He had already posted strong detachments at Dundalk, Ardee, Kells, Newry, and Carlingford, to keep them in awe on that side, while Sir Henry Dockwra, a brave English officer, was ordered to make a descent in Lough Foyle with four thousand men. This was effectually accomplished, Dockwra landing his forces in O'Dogherty's territory of Innishowen, and taking possession of Derry, with the forts of Culmore and Dunalong, all of which he greatly strengthened.

On the 5th of May, Mountjoy opened the campaign in person, and having reached Newry, received information that Tyrone had destroyed the fort of Portmor, set fire to Armagh, and then retired into the fastnesses of Lough Lurkin, where he had formed intrenchments and fortifications three miles in length. On the 15th the deputy marched towards Armagh, with seventeen hundred men, and on the 17th captain Blayney, with the advanced guard was attacked near the Pass of Moyry, by Tyrone, at the head of a considerable force; but by the opportune arrival of the deputy with his main body, the Irish chieftain was compelled to abandon the field. This event, with the establishment of the English forces at Lough Foyle, tended greatly to diminish Tyrone's power and consequence; many of his adherents deserted his cause, and Sir Arthur O'Neil with others of his chief partisans, sought for pardon and protection. But while the lord deputy was thus making successful progress in extinguishing the rebellion in Ulster, he was suddenly recalled to the capital by fresh outrages of the Leinster insurgents, who had lately released the earl of Ormond on his giving hostages for the payment of a large ransom. He immediately put his forces in motion in that direction, and pursued Tirrel and O'More into the

Queen's County, where the latter was killed in a bold attack which he made upon the royal army. In this expedition Mountjoy had the good fortune to rescue lord Ormond's hostages, and he subdued the last hopes of the rebels in this district, by reducing their country to a desert. Similar measures were adopted by Sir Arthur Chichester and Sir Samuel Bagnal, in the northern province, and thus the inhabitants being prevented from cultivating their lands, Tyrone with his dispirited army, shrunk gradually within narrower bounds, while famine, misery, and death, pervaded the whole surrounding district.

After having tranquillized Leinster as above related, Mountjoy early in September, again entered the northern province, and assembled at Dundalk a force of two thousand seven hundred men, with whom he marched on the 9th of October, to the Moyry Pass, which Tyrone had lately fortified with great care, and powerfully manned with soldiers. But the viceroy drove him from his intrenchments sword in hand, then advanced to Newry, eight miles beyond which he erected a new fort, named it Mount Norris, in honor of his master in the art of war, Sir John Norris, and placed it under the command of captain Blayney. He now offered a reward of two thousand pounds for the capture of the great rebel chieftain, and then retired to Carlingford, where Tyrone made another attack on his army, but was vigorously repulsed with the loss of two hundred men.

During these proceedings Red Hugh O'Donnel was indefatigable in his exertions against the English interests in Connaught and the western parts of Ulster. Having determined on another predatory incursion in Thomond, he had passed the river of Sligo for that purpose, when he received intelligence that his kinsman Neil O'Donnel *Garruffe*, (or the Boisterous,) with two of his brethren, had joined the English, and placed in their hands the castle of Lifford. Red Hugh immediately returned to Ulster and invested the fortress, which gave rise to a desultory warfare in this quarter, that continued for several months with little advantage on either side.

While the viceroy was thus successful in diminishing the power and influence of the insurgent lords of Ulster and Leinster, Sir George Carew had made considerable progress towards the re-establishment of the royal authority in the southern province. After receiving the submission of Fitzgerald and Power, two insurgent leaders at Waterford, he marched to Youghal, where he obtained information that Florence Mac Arthy, who had been lately raised up by government as rival to Daniel, in the chieftainship of his sept, had accepted the title of Mac Arthy More from the earl of Tyrone, and that he had a few days before manifested his attachment to the rebel cause by assembling a body of two thousand Irish, with which he attacked a division of the royal forces in a glen midway between Cork and Kinsale. The English who amounted to about thirteen hundred men, were driven back at the first onset of their antagonists under the walls of an old castle; but captain Flower, turning on his pursuers, charged them so briskly with his cavalry, that the Irish were finally routed with the loss of two hundred men.

When the president arrived in Cork, an official report of the state of the province was laid before him, from which it appeared that the spirit of disloyalty was so universal, that even the cities and great towns abounded with disaffected persons; and that besides the many thousands of their followers which the insurgent lords were able to bring into the field, they had employed five thousand Connaught mercenaries under Redmond Bourke and Dermod O'Connor. To encounter this formidable enemy, Carew commanded a force of not more than three thousand foot and two hundred and fifty horse, which he was well convinced must be wholly inadequate to the task of subduing his opponents, should they continue united. To create jealousy and suspicion of each other's fidelity amongst them was therefore the president's first object; and events soon proved how expert a master Sir George Carew was in all the arts of political dissimulation. He spread rumours of intended devastating excursions from his head-quarters, which compelled the neighbouring chieftains to submit to the royal mercy, and even Florence Mac Arthy consented to remain neutral. He next practised with O'Connor the chieftain of the Connaught mercenaries, who had married a daughter of the late earl of Desmond. This lady, having received an English education, was attached to the government, and naturally averse to the usurper of her brother's title; and through her influence O'Connor was prevailed on, for a sum of money, to deliver the titular earl into the hands of the president. After arranging these preliminaries, Sir George Carew declared his intention of marching towards Limerick on the 6th of May, and devastating all the lands and houses of the rebels on his route, which so alarmed the White Knight and some other chieftains, that they immediately sent in their submissions; while Pierce Lacy, the chief insurgent leader of Limerick, blew up his castle of Bruff, and Redmond Bourke returned to Connaught.

But notwithstanding these desertions, a large insurgent force was collected in the great wood of Kilmore, between Mallow and Kilmallock, to intercept Sir George in his march. The president, however, had too much sagacity to fall into this snare, and he deferred his journey till they had dispersed, when suddenly quitting Cork he reached Kilmallock without opposition. From hence he proceeded to Limerick, and commenced preparations for the siege of the castle of Lough-Gur; but this fortress was surrendered, before a shot was fired against it, by Groome, the governor, on a promise of pardon, and a reward of sixty pounds. Another incident occurred at this time which proves how little the associates in a bad cause can depend on each other. One Nugent, a servant of Sir Thomas Norris, the late lord president, had deserted to the rebels, and by his apparent devotedness to their service, had gained much of their confidence. Now that their affairs seemed declining, he expressed a wish to return to his allegiance, and made a proposal to the president of purchasing his pardon by destroying either the titular earl or his brother John. As Sir George Carew had already made arrangements with Dermod O'Connor for the seizure of the earl, he directed the attention of Nugent to his brother, and he accordingly attempted to dispatch John of Desmond while riding with him in the wood of Aherlow. He had just levelled a pistol at his intended victim, when he was seized, and condemned to die; and at his execution he confessed his design, adding that many others had sworn to the lord president to accomplish what he had intended; a declaration which so intimidated Desmond and his brother, that they were ever after afraid to lodge together, or appear at the head of their troops.

Dermod O'Connor's proposal of seizing the titular earl yet remained to be executed. To favour the design, the president, after devastating the lands of the insurgents in the county of Limerick, suddenly distributed his forces in the neighbouring towns, and the rebel chieftains followed his example. O'Connor, conceiving this to be the opportune moment for effecting his purpose, solicited an interview with the titular earl on the 18th of June, that they might deliberate on the posture of their affairs. Desmond accompanied by a son of lord Kerry attended the appointment; but in the midst of their conference O'Connor suddenly produced a letter purporting to have been written by the lord president to the earl, and which intimated that a secret correspondence existed between them. This letter O'Connor declared he had intercepted, and instantly seized Desmond as a traitor to the earl of Tyrone and his cause, and confined him with his attendants in Castle Ishin in the great wood of Connello. Intelligence of this important event was instantly transmitted to Sir George Carew; but before he could arrive to secure his prize, Castle Ishin was surrounded by four thousand men under lord Kerry, the knight of Glin, and Pierce Lacy, who speedily rescued the captives, while O'Connor found means to appease his associates.

Though his plans had not succeeded to the full extent of his wishes, yet the jealousies which they excited among the insurgent chieftains encouraged Sir George Carew to proceed with vigour in his military operations. He marched from Limerick early in July at the head of fifteen hundred men, captured Croom, a castle belonging to the earl of Kildare, and then invested the castle of Glin, which was strongly situated on the banks of the Shannon; Desmond, though encamped on a neighbouring eminence with double his force, not daring to attack him. The governor of Glin castle having refused to surrender, a child of the knight, aged six years, who had been for some time a hostage with the president, was placed on one of the gabions; but the garrison signifying that their fears for his life should not slacken their fire, he was removed from his perilous station, and the besiegers adopted more legitimate means for subduing the garrison. The vigorous fire of the English batteries having soon made a practicable breach in the castle, captain Flower with a party of his men entered the vault under the great hall, where he maintained his post until the following morning amidst showers of shot. The constable having attempted to escape in the night was slain, and the survivors of the garrison ascended to the battlements, declaring their firm resolution to sell their lives as dearly as possible. The English, under captains Flower and Slingsby, now mounted the narrow stairs in single file, and as each man reached the top he found himself engaged hand to hand with the enemy in that perilous situation : a dreadful conflict ensued, in which the still increasing numbers of the assailants at length succeeded. The remnant of the garrison, amounting to eighty men, were either slain by the sword, or precipitated from the battlements into the Shannon, while on the part of the English nearly half that number were killed or wounded.

Desmond and his confederates now fled into Kerry, while O'Connor returned into his own country with the Connaught mercenaries. The president followed up his success by capturing the castle of Carrigfoyle, from whence he sent Maurice Stack into Kerry at the head of a small detachment. Stack was a native of this county, and though a man of remarkably small stature, he possessed great activity and invincible courage. With his handful of men he marched into the heart of the country, set fire to the town of Ardfert, and surprised Liscahan castle, which he maintained against all the force and wiles of lord Kerry and Florence Mac Arthy, till the president and the earl of Thomond arrived to its relief. Six hundred men under Sir Charles Wilmot were now detached against lord Kerry's castle of Lixnaw, which they captured, and then pushed forward to regain the castle of Tralee which Desmond had just taken from Sir Edward Denny. Wilmot reached it at the moment when the enemy were preparing to blow it up: a number of the Irish were put to the sword, and the remainder fled to the mountains of Slievemish.—The knight of Kerry about this time abandoned the cause of the insurgents, and refused the mock earl admission into his castle of Dingle. Desmond set fire to the town before his departure, and he with Pierce Lacy returned soon after to plunder his lands: but the knight gave them such a warm reception, that they were compelled to fly with the loss of two of their principal officers and several of their followers.

The capture of his chief castle of Lixnaw so preyed on the mind of lord Kerry, that he died of grief a few days after. His son and successor Thomas, who was now in his twenty-sixth year, had married a sister of the earl of Thomond, but he rejected every effort made by his noble kinsman to induce him to return to his allegiance. His lady appears to have indulged similar sentiments, and she formed a plan for avenging the death of her father-in-law on one of the chief partisans of the English government in this country. About the end of August she invited the brave Maurice Stack to dine with her at her lord's castle of Beaulieu. After dinner she desired to speak with him privately in her chamber, where a disagreement having taken place between them, she called out to some of her adherents who were stationed at the door, "*Do you not hear him abuse me?*" The assassins instantly rushed in, stabbed Stack with their skeins, and threw him out of a high window into the court-yard: his brother Thomas Stack was hanged by lord Kerry on the following day, by which he manifested his participation in the foul murder.—The earl of Thomond would never see his sister after the commission of this detestable crime, nor did she survive it a year.

Desmond's affairs appeared now so desperate,

that he was abandoned by his principal associates. His brother John, with Pierce Lacy, fled into Ulster; Florence Mac Arthy returned to his neutral position, and the titular earl himself became a fugitive, exposed, like his unfortunate predecessor, to continual perils. On the 16th of September, while passing at the head of the scanty remnant of his forces, from Connello to the wood of Aherlow, he was attacked by a detachment of the garrison of Kilmallock, commanded by Sir George Thornton, and defeated with the loss of two hundred men, and all his baggage. Soon after this event, the government adopted a plan for dividing his followers and distracting his counsels, by setting up a rival to his power, in the person of James, the son of that earl of Desmond who had been the first promoter of the rebellion in Munster. Lord James Fitzgerald had been educated in England, and was kept in the tower of London in a kind of honorable seclusion. He was now released, saluted as the earl of Desmond, and sent over to Ireland; the patent for his restoration being placed in the hands of the lord president, to be delivered or retained as circumstances might require. Sir George Carew received the young earl at Mallow, and immediately forwarded him to the county of Limerick, under the conduct of the archbishop of Cashel, and Mr. Boyle, afterwards the great earl of Cork. When he arrived at Kilmallock, the chief town of his ancestors, he was received with extraordinary demonstrations of joy, the inhabitants throwing upon him wheat and salt, a ceremony used in the election of their magistrates as a token of future peace and plenty. The windows and roofs of the houses were crowded with spectators, anxious to catch a glimpse of the heir of their ancient lords; while a guard of soldiers with difficulty made a passage for the earl through the dense multitude which thronged the streets, and rent the air with their acclamations. But on the following day, which was Sunday, the streets of Kilmallock presented a very different scene. The young lord, who was educated in the principles of the established church, proceeded to attend divine service through a similar concourse as that which had attended him on the preceding day.

But the tone and language of the populace were completely changed: they thundered in his ears the disgrace, danger, and impropriety of forsaking the religion of his ancestors, and joining in the heretical worship; and on his return from church he was greeted with loud insults and execrations. During his future residence in Ireland, he remained unnoticed and unattended—and being unable to render any material service to the government, he returned to England, where he died in the following year.

The want of success that attended the restoration of young Desmond, was now of the less importance, as the affairs of the Munster rebels appeared to be reduced to the lowest ebb. Tyrone was too closely pressed by the vigilant Mountjoy to be able to render any assistance, while their Connaught auxiliaries had either made their peace with the government, or found it necessary for the present to temporize. Their late ally, Dermod O'Connor, on learning that his brother-in-law, the young earl of Desmond, had arrived in Munster, obtained a safe-conduct from the president to join him with a body of his followers; but in passing through O'Shaughnessy's country, about eighteen miles from Limerick, he was attacked by Theobald-ny-lung Bourke, who was captain of a hundred foot in the queen's service.— O'Connor took refuge in an old church, which Bourke set on fire; and as the soldiers were issuing from the flames, he slew forty of them, and took O'Connor prisoner, whom he beheaded on the following day, in revenge, he said, for the death of his cousin lord Bourke. The government were so incensed at this act, that Theobald Bourke was dismissed from her majesty's service.

All the strong holds of the insurgents of Munster had now fallen into the hands of the royal forces, with the exception of the castle of Listowel, belonging to lord Kerry, to which Sir Charles Wilmot laid siege on the fifth of November. The fortress being soon undermined, the garrison surrendered, and were all put to death as traitors, having formerly received protections, with the exception of a priest named Mac Brodie, whose life was saved on the following account. So confident was lord Kerry in the impregnable strength of Listowel castle, that he deposited there not only his most valuable goods, but his eldest son, a child five years old. Anxious for the safety of their young charge, the unfortunate garrison, though despairing of life for themselves, disarrayed him of his accustomed dress, smeared his face with dirt, and committed him to the care of an old woman, who conveyed him, naked and disfigured, on her back through the hostile encampment. Sir Charles Wilmot, when he learned the circumstance, searched in vain for the prize which had escaped him. He then threatened the priest with instant death unless he disclosed to him the place of the infant's concealment; but this the priest refused to do till Sir Charles gave him assurance that his own life and that of the child should be spared. He then conducted a party of soldiers to a wood about six miles distant from the castle, where, in a cave whose entrance was completely concealed by thorns and briars nearly impenetrable, the little innocent and his faithful nurse were found; and the child was immediately sent to the lord president, and retained as a hostage for the future fidelity of his father. The anxiety thus manifested by the unfortunate garrison of Listowel, even in the immediate prospect of death, to preserve the infant heir of their lord, affords a fine trait of that fidelity and attachment to their leaders which have in all ages marked the Irish character.

The spirit of the insurgents seemed now completely broken, and their wretched chief chose the life of a wandering kern rather than commit himself to the protection of any of his confederates. The president sent out detachments of military, which soon rendered that part of the county of Limerick where the miserable remains of the rebel forces had taken refuge a complete desert, and above four thousand persons laid down their arms and submitted to the queen's mercy. A royal pardon was issued to any of the southern rebels who should be recommended by the lord president, with the exception of the titular earl of Desmond, his brother John, Pierce Lacy, lord Kerry, and the knight of Glin, or the Valley.

Though a death-like tranquillity now prevailed throughout Munster, yet the vigilant Carew was aware that the most active exertions were being made to re-animate the spirit of insubordination in the South, both by the foreign and domestic enemies of the English government. Oviedo, a Spanish ecclesiastic, who had been lately appointed by the pope archbishop of Dublin, gave strong assurances of the speedy arrival of Spanish succours, while Tyrone received fresh letters from the Holy Father, filled with benedictions on him and all his faithful adherents *who had not bowed the knee to Baal;* and the great northern leader sent emissaries among the disaffected in the other provinces, to prepare them for the reception of their foreign allies. Carew, therefore, saw the necessity of redoubled exertions for the apprehension of the principal southern chieftain, which had hitherto been prevented by the fidelity of the followers of that unhappy lord, who resisted every temptation that the promise of security and wealth afforded. But in the month of May, 1601, an incident occurred, which ultimately led to the accomplishment of the president's desire.

A party of lord Barry's soldiers pursued some robbers into a wood where Desmond was concealed with a few companions. Alarmed at their approach, the chieftain started from the miserable supper which had been prepared for him, and fled to the territory of Fitzgibbon, the White Knight, while a mantle, which he left behind, discovered to the soldiers the valuable prize which had just escaped them.

Lord Barry, who was at this time at variance with the White Knight, imputed Desmond's escape to the negligence or treachery of that chieftain, who, being under protection, was threatened by the president that his life and lands should be made accountable if the fugitive were not secured. Stung by these reproaches, and alarmed by the danger with which he was menaced, the White Knight declared that he would bring in Desmond dead or alive; and having offered a reward of fifty pounds for his apprehension, he was led by one of his followers, accompanied by six or seven men, to a cave in the mountain of Slieugort, in Tipperary.—The party entered the cave, with their swords drawn, and there found the unhappy object of their pursuit, accompanied only by his foster-brother. They submitted without resistance, and Desmond was instantly sent to Cork, where he was tried and convicted of high treason: but Sir George Carew recommended that his life should be spared, as otherwise his brother John might assume the title, and become equally dangerous to the state. He was accordingly sent to London, and confined in the tower till his death, which occurred in 1608. His brother John, who had escaped to Spain, then assumed the title, in which he was succeeded by his only son Gerald, who after serving with distinction in the armies of Germany and Spain, died without issue in 1632, and with him ended the last hope of this illustrious but turbulent family.

CHAPTER XIII.

Vigorous Proceedings of Lord Mountjoy in Ulster — Action at Benburb — Landing of Spanish Troops at Kinsale under Don Juan de Aquila—Advance of the Viceroy against the Invaders—Siege of Kinsale—March of Tyrone and O'Donnel to the South—Fresh Disembarkation of Spaniards at Castlehaven —Perilous state of the English Army—Battle of Kinsale and Flight of the Irish Chieftains — Death of Red Hugh O'Donnel — Surrender of Kinsale—Obstinate Defence of the Castle of Dunboy by O'Sullivan Beare— Death of M‘Egan, the Apostolic Vicar — Perilous Flight of O'Sullivan, O'Connor Kerry, &c.—Defeat and Death of Captain Malby—Singular Preservation of O'Sullivan's Family—Story of Teig Keugh Mac Mahon and Henry O'Brien of Trummera—The Viceroy's Progress in Ulster—Final Overthrow and Submission of Tyrone—Death of Queen Elizabeth.

WHILE the lord president of Munster was thus successful in crushing the southern insurrection, the viceroy Mountjoy continued the most vigorous exertions for the reduction of the great northern chieftain. On the 22d of May 1601, he marched from Dublin, and after adopting various regulations for the security of the district through which he passed, reached Armagh on the 23d of June, which the Irish abandoned at his approach. He advanced to the Blackwater on the 13th of July, and after an action of three hours' continuance drove Tyrone from his intrenchments at Benburb with considerable loss, and proceeded to erect a new fort on the ruins of Portmor. But while engaged in these operations, Tyrone's forces suddenly appeared in an adjacent meadow, and raising a loud shout, which was mingled with the noise of drums and bag-pipes, fired several thousand shot into the viceroy's camp. Mountjoy had anticipated such a visit by planting four hundred men in ambush, who now poured on

Tyrone's forces such an unexpected and destructive volley, that they fled, leaving the ground covered with their slain, amongst whom was the celebrated southern chieftain Pierce Lacy of Bruff in the county of Limerick.

But the landing of a body of Spanish troops in Munster soon rendered the northern war an object of minor consideration. This event had been for some time anticipated by the leaders of the insurgents, who held various consultations as to the most suitable point for their disembarkation, and other matters necessary to their success. Limerick was at first proposed, on account of its proximity to Connaught and Leinster: but, at the suggestion of Florence Mac Arthy, Cork was ultimately fixed upon, as it contained the government stores, and was less capable of defence. The vigilant Carew being soon apprised of these proceedings, took the most prompt measures to meet the threatened danger. He demanded six thousand additional troops from England for the defence of his province, secured the person of Florence Mac Arthy, whom he sent into England, and imprisoned many others of the insurgent leaders, one of whom, after making strong professions of loyalty, justified the president's precaution when he suddenly asked him the question, " What would you do if the Spaniards should arrive?" " In that case," answered the chief, " let not your lordship confide in me ; no, nor in any of those lords who seem most devoted to your service."

The fears of the government were soon realized, for on the 22d of September seventeen Spanish ships of war and thirty-three transports were descried off Cork harbour, and on the following day Don Juan d'Aquila landed at Kinsale with five thousand troops, and took possession of the town, and the castle of Rincurran, without resistance. The Spanish general immediately sent despatches to Ulster to notify his arrival, and press the immediate march of Tyrone and O'Donnel to his support ; while foreign ecclesiastics spread themselves through the country in all directions to excite the people to revolt. On the first certain intimation of the invasion, Mountjoy had given up his pursuit of the northern insurgents, and after securing his conquests with sufficient garrisons, he marched southward with the remainder of his forces.

The arrival of two thousand troops from England increased the royal army to nearly eight thousand men, at whose head lord Mountjoy, after holding a conference with Sir George Carew at Kilkenny, advanced against the invaders, whose numbers were as yet little augmented by the natives, who were either intimidated by the vigorous preparations of the president, or disgusted by the coldness with which their overtures were received by their foreign allies. On the 17th of October the viceroy encamped at Knockrobbin, within half a mile of Kinsale, and from this period constant hostilities were kept up between the besiegers and the garrison, with considerable loss on both sides, till the 31st, when the castle of Rincurran, being rendered untenable by the English batteries, surrendered, and the Spanish garrison were sent prisoners to Cork.

The viceroy was now advancing in the siege with the most sanguine hopes of success, when intelligence arrived that Tyrone and O'Donnel were marching rapidly to the assistance of the

Spaniards. Red Hugh, on learning that his long expected friends had at length arrived, suddenly ceased his operations against Neil O'Donnel and the English of Donegal, and assembled all the forces he could collect, amounting to more than four thousand, at Ballymote, with whom he proceeded southwards on the 2d of November, and he halted during several weeks at Holy Cross in Tipperary, waiting for Tyrone's troops, who were slowly advancing. Mountjoy thinking it prudent to attempt the destruction of O'Donnel's force before this junction should be effected, Sir George Carew was despatched with about three thousand men, with whom he marched rapidly to Ardmaile within four miles of O'Donnel's camp; but the latter, favoured by a severe frost, passed over the mountain of Slievephelim into the county of Limerick, and crossing bogs and morasses that would have otherwise proved impassable, he ultimately reached Bandon, where he was soon after joined by the northern forces under Tyrone.

After a fruitless pursuit, the lord president returned to the camp at Kinsale, where he was consoled for his disappointment by finding that the royal army had been reinforced by more than five thousand men, under the earls of Thomond and Clanrickard, and Sir Richard Leviston. Lord Mountjoy was thus enabled to press the siege with augmented vigour.— The fort of Castlepark was compelled to submit; but when the Spanish commander was again summoned to surrender the town, he replied that he held it for Christ and the king of Spain; that he would maintain it against all their enemies, and, with a spirit of romantic valour for which his nation was then remarkable, he challenged the viceroy to decide the quarrel of their respective sovereigns by single combat.

Events, however, soon occurred, which tended to depress the hopes of the royal commanders, and raise the spirits of the foreigners. Six Spanish ships had landed two thousand additional troops at Castlehaven: further reinforcements were expected, while O'Donnel had united his forces with these new invaders. This appearance of powerful support encouraged many of the Munster chieftains who had hitherto remained neutral to throw off the mask, and the majority of the inhabitants of the counties of Cork, Limerick, and Kerry, declared for the Spaniards, to whom the O'Driscols surrendered their forts at Castlehaven and Baltimore.—O'Sullivan Beare received a Spanish garrison into his strong castle of Dunboy, while O'Connor Kerry placed Carrigfoyle in the hands of the foreigners, who put the whole garrison to the sword.

On the 2d of December, Kinsale was completely invested by the royal forces, and a vigorous cannonade was commenced on the 9th. But the English army had now a new enemy to contend with, Tyrone having taken post about six miles distance from their camp so as to cut off all intercourse with Cork, while O'Donnel and the Spaniards at Castlehaven pressed them on the opposite side. Thus the besiegers were in effect besieged in their turn; and being prevented from foraging, soon became in such want of provisions in the depth of winter, that many of them dropped dead on their posts, numbers deserted, and their losses were so scantily supplied from

England, that had Tyrone's advice been followed which recommended that the Irish and their allies should remain obstinately in their present situation, there is little doubt that the army on which the fate of the English power n Ireland seemed to depend, must have been speedily destroyed. But Don Juan, impatient of the long imprisonment which he had suffered in Kinsale, and confident of victory, solicited the Irish chieftains in the most urgent manner to attack the English camp, assuring them that he would at the same time make a vigorous sortie from the town; and from this joint effort he anticipated an easy triumph over an enemy already much weakened by famine and sickness.

At a council of war which was held by the confederate chieftains, Tyrone gave his decided opinion for the continuance of that system of blockade which they had hitherto so successfully pursued; but the ardent and enterprising O'Donnel declared for more active measures as a duty which they owed to their ally the king of Spain. His opinion prevailed, and after Tyrone had given a reluctant consent, the two chiefs, instead of cordially uniting in deliberating on the wisest mode of attack, are said to have spent a great part of the night in an altercation about precedence. Still they appeared so confident of victory, that we are told they argued whose prisoners the lord deputy and lord president should be.

Mountjoy, having received secret intelligence of all these proceedings from Mac Mahon, one of the insurgent chiefs, resolved to march against the advancing enemy, whose object was to throw a strong reinforcement into the town during the assault of the royal position. Having accordingly charged the lord president with the defence of the camp against Don Juan, he proceeded on the morning of the 24th of December with sixteen hundred men against the confederate Irish, whom he found advantageously posted. But the English horse, under marshal Wingfield and the earl of Clanrickard, having crossed a bog behind which a large body of the enemy were stationed, the latter were speedily broken and fled. The remainder of the army, as if struck with a panic, followed the example, with the exception of the Spaniards and the vanguard under Tyrrel, who gallantly maintained their ground for some time, till they were entirely broken, and Ocampo, the Spanish general, was taken prisoner by a charge of lord Mountjoy's horse under Sir William Godolphin. In this singular action the English are said to have had but one cornet slain, and five or six officers with some twenty or thirty common soldiers wounded, while of the Irish twelve hundred fell in the battle or pursuit, and eight hundred were wounded, lord Clanrickard we are told, slaying with his own hand, no less than twenty. It might be compared to the *Battle of the Spurs*, which Henry the VIII. fought at Guinegate in Picardy, where the French cavaliers trusted more to their spurs than to their swords. But it is scarcely accountable on natural principles, that men distinguished by so much skill and bravery as Tyrone and O'Donnel had displayed for so many years, should now at the head of six or seven thousand troops, exhibit such pusillanimity before a handful of men greatly inferior in number, and much reduced by their sufferings in physical strength.

Tyrone fled with the remnant of his followers to his own territory in the North, while O'Donnel embarked for Spain to solicit fresh succours. He was received at Corunna with the highest honours by count Caracena, who accompanied him to court, where the king treated him with the greatest affability, and promised to fulfil all his requests. At St. James of Compostella he was received with great magnificence by the clergy and citizens; and the archbishop, after celebrating mass with much solemnity, administered the sacrament to the Irish chieftain. The archbishop then entertained him at dinner, and at his departure presented him with a thousand ducats. He remained at Corunna for several months in expectation of the promised succours from the king: but, while on a second journey to the court, he was carried off by a sudden illness in the 32d year of his age, and thus terminated the active and turbulent life of Red Hugh O'Donnel. All who read his history must regret that his great talents and energies were not better directed; for though it must be freely admitted that his resentment against the

English government was at first excited by the most cruel injustice, yet he afterwards carried it to an unwarrantable length, which brought ruin on himself and inflicted dreadful misery on his country.

After the English army had returned to the camp before Kinsale they offered public thanksgivings to heaven for a victory which had been unexpectedly gained with so little loss on the part of the conquerors; and they afterwards gave a striking proof of their gratitude by subscribing £1800 to commence a Library in Trinity College, Dublin, which had been founded about ten years before. It was a large sum in those days to be contributed by so small an army; and with this money the celebrated archbishop Ussher went to London to purchase the books which served as the nucleus of that splendid library which at this day confers so much honor on the university and the nation.

When Don Juan heard the volleys which the besiegers discharged in honor of their triumph, he conceived them to be signals of the approach of his Irish allies, and instantly sallied from the town to meet them. But the sight of the

Spanish colours, in possession of the English, soon undeceived him, and he made a precipitate retreat. When informed of the circumstances of the battle, the indignation of Don Juan against his allies seemed unbounded, and he solicited an immediate parley with the lord deputy. Sir William Godolphin was appointed to confer with him, to whom he intimated his wish for a termination of hostilities on such terms as should be consistent with his honour. Sir William proposed that he should surrender all the places which he held in Ireland to the lord deputy, who would allow him to hire and victual ships to transport his forces into their own country: but that all his treasure, ordnance, and ammunition, should be left at the absolute disposal of the queen of England.—The last article was rejected with disdain by Don Juan, who declared that he would sooner meet the viceroy on the breach than consent to it. He was anxious, he said, to conclude the business on honourable terms, for he had seen the condes O'Neil and O'Donnel, whom the king his master had sent him to assist, assemble their utmost force within two miles of Kinsale, and that force broken by a handful of men, blown asunder into different parts of the world —O'Donnel into Spain—O'Neil into the furthest part of Ulster—so that he could not find such condes *in rerum naturæ*.

As his army had been diminished during the siege by more than six thousand men, while fresh succours were daily expected from Spain by the enemy, Mountjoy deemed it prudent, under all circumstances, to withdraw the obnoxious article, and early in January, 1602, the negociation was brought to a conclusion.— Kinsale, Castlehaven, and Baltimore, were surrendered to the English, and arrangements made for conveying the remnant of the Spanish army, amounting to 3027 men, to their own country. At these proceedings some of the southern chieftains were highly incensed; and when captain Flower was approaching to take possession of the castle of Dunboy at Bearhaven, Daniel O'Sullivan Beare laid a plan for recovering it from the hands of the Spaniards, that he might afterwards defend it against the royal forces. Though he had delivered the custody of the castle to his foreign allies, he frequently

lodged therein with some of his followers.—
One night, while the Spaniards were fast asleep,
he caused some of his trusty adherents to break
a hole in the wall, through which fourscore
Irish soldiers entered, and when day dawned
the garrison were astonished to see a thousand
men drawn up in the neighbourhood of the
castle, commanded by lord Kerry, Tyrrel, and
William Bourke, and accompanied by Archer
the Jesuit and another priest. At the instigation of Archer, Saavedra, the Spanish governor, was induced to relinquish his charge, and he with his garrison embarked at Baltimore.

When Don Juan was informed of this affair, he, with that sense of honor by which the Spaniards were then so much distinguished, offered his services to reduce Dunboy before his departure; but he was told that the queen's officers would take care to chastise the rebels, and Sir George Carew made speedy preparations for that purpose. The earl of Thomond was despatched with thirteen hundred men into Carbery, to ascertain the movements of the insurgents, and having proceeded as far as the abbey of Bantry, he brought information that O'Sullivan, assisted by two Spanish engineers and a friar named Dominick Collins, was actively engaged in fortifying the castle of Dunboy, of which Richard M'Geoghegan, a distinguished Irish officer, was appointed governor, while the troops under Tyrrel defended the passes of the mountains.

Having previously despatched Sir Charles Wilmot into Kerry to crush the remaining symptoms of insurrection in that district, Sir George Carew proceeded with fifteen hundred men along the sea-cost to Bantry, where he had to wait a considerable time for the shipping to convey him to Bearhaven, as the way by land was impassable for an army. Here he was joined by Sir Charles Wilmot after a perilous march over Mangerton mountain, in which Tyrrel and O'Sullivan endeavoured in vain to impede his progress. The army was now transported by sea to Bearhaven, and in the beginning of June the president sat down before Dunboy, which was so strong both by nature and art, that the Irish deemed it impregnable, while it was defended by a garrison enthusiastically devoted to the cause which they had embraced, and whose zeal was continually animated by the energetic exhortations of father Collins, their chaplain. The president soon perceived that he had obstacles to encounter of no ordinary nature, yet he vigorously pressed the siege in the face of a tremendous fire from the fortress, while his camp was harassed night and day by the desultory attacks of Tyrrel and O'Sullivan. At length the English batteries beat down one of the principal towers of the castle, and the breach, after a determined resistance, was entered by a gallant band, under lieutenants Kirton and Meutas, who planted the president's colours on a turret of the barbican. The brave M'Geoghegan, still undismayed, retired with the remnant of his garrison to another tower, which he had encircled with a rampart of earth, from whence they kept up a murderous fire of hail-shot upon the assailants. But the latter still pressed forward with undaunted intrepidity, and the principal gunner of the castle having fallen by a chance-shot, while the south-east tower was entered by captain

Slingsby, the Irish retreated to a narrow passage in the east of the castle, which they defended for a considerable time against all the force of the assailants. About forty of the besieged, who had sallied out of the castle towards the sea, were nearly all put to the sword. Seventy-seven still remained with their commander M'Geoghegan, who was soon mortally wounded by a shower of bullets which the English poured down the staircase. Father Collins and twenty-five others now surrendered: the remainder of the garrison, however, being still resolved to hold out, appointed one Taylor their captain, who, seating himself with a lighted brand in the midst of nine barrels of gunpowder, vowed to blow up the castle and all its inmates unless their lives were secured to them. But Sir George Carew, unintimidated by this threat, ordered a new battery to be erected against the vault, and as soon as the balls began to fly among them, Taylor was compelled by his comrades to submit. Sir George Thornton now entering the vault to secure the prisoners, M'Geoghegan, who was still alive, seized a lighted candle, which he was about to apply to an open barrel of gunpowder, when he was seized by captain Power, who held him in his arms till he was killed. The remnant of the brave garrison, fifty-eight in number, were executed on the same day; and none of the Irish survived this gallant defence except father Collins, Taylor, M'Sweeny, and two or three others, but they afterwards underwent a similar fate at Cork and Youghal.

The castle of Dunboy being now demolished, O'Sullivan, who had long borne the title of prince of Beare and Bantry, became a fugitive, with his wife and family, in the wood of Glengarriff, while Tyrrel and O'Connor Kerry kept up a communication with him across the ridges of Slievelogher; and M'Egan, the apostolic vicar, from his asylum among the Mac Arthys of Carberry, thundered out his excommunications against all heretics, till he fell, mortally wounded, in a skirmish with the royal forces. But the unceasing activity of Sir Charles Wilmot soon deprived the unfortunate O'Sullivan of his last refuge in Munster. The remnant of his scattered forces were driven from mountain to mountain, and from rock to rock, till they were nearly cut off, while scarcely a cow, a sheep, or a garran was left to him from Slievemish to Glenflesk. With famine staring him and his followers in the face, at the approach of winter, or the alternative of an ignominious death by the hands of the executioner, he resolved still to preserve a life which he had devoted to the Catholic cause, by flying to Ulster with Tyrrel, William Bourke, O'Connor Kerry, and about one hundred of his veteran followers. They commenced their perilous journey in the depth of winter, and having taken their way through the Murdering Glen, and arrived at the foot of the Ivelearagh mountains, they entered Muskerry, where, being attacked by Teige Mac Arthy at the passage of the Lee, they lost some of their best men. Barry of Buttevant turned upon the unhappy fugitives the guns of the castle of Liscarrol, and pursued them till, passing the Ballyhoura mountains, they descended into the plains of Limerick, where for a few days they found quiet refreshment for themselves and their horses.

Thence they proceeded northwards through

the Galtees, till they entered the rich valley of the Suir, where they had hoped to meet a welcome from the opulent abbeys which raised their cloistered fronts along the banks of that beautiful river. But when arrived at the Rock of Cashel, learning that the sheriff of the palatinate of Tipperary was on horse with all his force for their destruction, they fled along the plain between the Suir and the mountains of Clanwilliam. After receiving some refreshment from the monks of Monaincha, they marched under Benduff, from whence the Suir and Nore take their rise, and proceeding by the borders of Ormond and Ely O'Carrol, at length reached the Shannon, near the old abbey of Terryglass. But finding that the sheriff of Tipperary, with a large force, was within a few miles of them, while the Shannon spread before them like a sea to obstruct their progress, O'Sullivan proposed that they should slaughter their horses, and make corraghs, or basket-boats of their skins, to transport them beyond the reach of their enemies. This was speedily accomplished; and when the sheriff and his train arrived, they perceived, to their great disappointment, O'Sullivan and his little troop afloat on the bosom of the Shannon.

The fugitives effected a landing in Galway, at a place then called Tough-Kilnalehen, and here they remained as long as their horse-flesh lasted. They then proceeded towards Clanrickard, where they were opposed by Sir Thomas Bourke and Captain Malby, at the head of a party of the royal forces. O'Sullivan and his confederates took post in a rocky fortress, well protected, to which the only accessible avenue was a narrow defile overhung with wood. Malby, with that impetuosity of character for which he was remarkable, rushed fearlessly into the defile, when O'Connor Kerry, who had been his acquaintance in more peaceable times, exclaimed, " Malby, my old friend, come not a foot farther, or you are a dead man. I have you covered with my good arquebuss, which never missed its aim. I once gave you my hand in friendship—that hand would be reluctantly raised to send you into eternity. Why seek our lives? Let us pass to O'Rourke's country in peace, and not a cow or a garran of yours will we touch." " Down, rebels, with your arms, and submit to the queen's clemency!" was the only reply of the fiery Malby. "Clemency!" exclaimed O'Sullivan, "O, ye spirits of my people, murdered in cold blood at Dunboy, bear witness to Saxon clemency!—Fire! fire!—in memory of Dunboy. Hurra, O'Sullivan aboo! fire!" A well directed volley was discharged; Malby with some of his bravest men fell dead; the remainder of the royal forces took to flight, and O'Sullivan and his confederates fought their passage into O'Rourke's country.

A tradition prevails, that when O'Sullivan was quitting his retreat in Glengarriff, he consigned the care of his wife and children to a faithful gossip named Gorrane Mac Swiney, who had a hut at the foot of the Eagle's Precipice, which was so constructed as to elude the vigilance of the English scouts who, day and night, prowled about these mountains. A single salted salmon was all the provision which Mac Swiney had for his honoured charge when they entered his hut, but his ingenuity is said to have devised extraordinary means for their future sustenance. Having perceived an eagle flying to her nest with a hare in her talons, he conceived a plan for supporting the family of his chief with the food intended for the young eaglets. He accordingly, on the following morning, accompanied by his son, a boy about fourteen years old, ascended the mountains, on the summit of which they took post till they saw the old eagles fly off in pursuit of prey. The elder Mac Swiney then tied a rope made of the fibres of bog fir round the waist and between the legs of his son, and lowered him down to the nest, where the youth tightened the necks of the young eaglets with straps which he had provided for the purpose, that they might swallow their food with difficulty. This being accomplished, he was safely drawn up, and the father and son kept their station on the top of the precipice, till they witnessed the return of the eagles—one with a rabbit, and the other with a grouse in its talons. After they had again flown off, young Mac Swiney descended a second time, and brought up the game, after having first gutted it, and left the entrails for the young eaglets. In this manner, we are informed, was the family of O'Sullivan supported by their faithful guardian, during the period of their seclusion in this desolate part of the country.

This dreadful civil war was, no doubt, productive of many events of deep and romantic interest, which have been suffered to sink into oblivion; but one still remains to us which is worthy of being recorded. Near the mouth of the Shannon, on the Clare side of the river, stands the ruined castle of Carrigaholt, which with the whole peninsula of West Corkavaskin, was long the property of the ancient sept of Mac Mahon. Teig Keugh Mac Mahon, its last proprietor of that name, being connected by marriage with Lord Kerry, became implicated in the rebellion against Elizabeth, and spent most of his time with the army on the opposite side of the river, leaving his wife and an unmarried daughter in the castle of Carrigaholt. Complaints having been made to the earl of Thomond of some outrages committed by Mac Mahon, of whose connexion with the rebels the earl was then ignorant, he sent his brother, Henry O'Brien of Trummera Castle, to Carrigaholt, to remonstrate with the chieftain. MacMahon was at this time absent; but young

O'Brien was soon so captivated by the charms of his daughter, that he appears to have forgotten the object of his embassy, and spent three weeks at the castle, dividing his time between the pleasures of the chase and the society of the fair object of his attachment. The young lady, however, knowing her father's rooted hostility to the Thomond family, not only despaired of his ever consenting to her union with O'Brien, but even dreaded that he would assassinate him, should he find him at the castle on his return. She therefore agreed, that if her father should arrive during his periodical absence, she would notify the circumstance by hoisting a black handkerchief on the western pinnacle of the fortress.

The castle of Carrigaholt was enclosed by a court-yard, secured by high walls on one side, and by the bay with its high cliffs on the other, from which to the White Strand, on the Moyarta side of the creek, there is a passage several hundred yards in depth. Henry O'Brien, returning from the chase one evening, was so absorbed in thought, that he neglected to look towards the pinnacle, till the shutting of the gate behind him aroused him from his reverie, and he beheld the fatal signal waving in mournful undulations. His followers, except one, were instantly secured; but to the astonishment of Mac Mahon, the intrepid O'Brien and his faithful servant plunged with their horses into the foaming tide, from the Black Rock near the castle; and, under a heavy fire from the assassins, arrived safely on the white strand of Moyarta. A detachment of Mac Mahon's men had, in the mean time, hurried round to a cliff, from whence, firing a volley on the fugitives, they killed O'Brien's servant, and wounded himself severely in one of his hands. He escaped, however, and the earl of Thomond sent him soon after to the court of Elizabeth, with his arm in a sling, where he represented the treachery of his insidious relative in such glowing colours, that Mac Mahon was declared an outlaw, and his entire estate granted to the injured O'Brien. In the mean time Mac Mahon was assassinated by his son Tirlagh during the siege of Dunboy, and the murderer having fled to Spain, Henry O'Brien got peaceable possession of the fair object of his wishes, with the castle of Carrigaholt, and the vast estate of West Corkavaskin, and became the founder of the Clare branch of the house of Thomond, which became so conspicuous in the subsequent history of Ireland.

Since the surrender of Kinsale, the viceroy Mountjoy had proceeded with vigour in completing the pacification of Ulster. After his discomfiture in the south, Tyrone, as already stated, fled to his own territories near the Blackwater, whither Mountjoy pursued him at the head of a considerable force, in the following June. Sir Richard Moryson having passed through Armagh, established himself on the north side of the river, and the viceroy erected a bridge and built a fort, which, after his own Christian-name, he called Charlemont, and of which sir Toby Caulfield, the founder of the Charlemont family, was the first governor. Tyrone was now pursued to his head-quarters at Dungannon; but the chieftain, on the approach of the royal forces, set fire to the town and his own mansion-house, and took refuge in Castle-Roe on the Bann. After this the viceroy spent some time in building

Mountjoy-fort on Lough Neagh, planting garrisons about Lough Foyle, and giving instructions to Maguire and Mac Mahon, the chieftains of Fermanagh and Monaghan, who had now become sincerely attached to the interests of the government.

Tyrone, having escaped from Castle-Roe with a small body of infantry and sixty horse, strongly entrenched himself at the extreme head of a glen near Lough Erne, while the whole of the surrounding country was abandoned to the devastation of the enraged royalists. In the month of June the English captured his great magazine at Magherlowny; and on the 10th of August the strong fort of Ennishlaghlin, situated in the midst of a deep bog, and surrounded with woods and artificial obstacles which rendered it nearly inaccessible, was stormed by Sir Arthur Chichester and Sir Henry Danvers, who found there a vast quantity of plate and other valuable articles belonging to the rebel chieftain. Lord Mountjoy then advanced to Dungannon, Tyrone's principal residence, of which he took possession, and at Tulloghoge, broke in pieces the stone chair of state, in which from the most remote antiquity the sovereigns of Ulster had been inaugurated into the regal dignity and authority of the O'Neil. Mr. Stuart, from whose truly valuable History of Armagh I have derived much of my information respecting the affairs of this province, states, that some fragments of this chair were found about sixty years ago in the neighbourhood of Dungannon.

This vigorous commander seemed now determined to put an end to the rebellion at every risk, and till that was accomplished to steel his breast against all compassion for the miseries of the unhappy victims of their great leader's ambition. The country was ravaged by the enraged soldiery, till all means of subsistence for its wretched inhabitants being destroyed, they were forced to the most horrible resources for allaying their hunger, and thousands perished by famine. You will be better able to judge of the terrible effects of this cruel civil war, when you learn that even in the city of Dublin, though far removed from the scene of hostilities, the price of wheat rose in 1602, from 36s. to £9. per quarter, a carcase of beef from 26s. 8d. to £8, and all other articles of provision in the same proportion.

Driven to despair by the unremitting vigour and severity of the viceroy, Rory O'Donnel, Sir Arthur O'Neil, and other subordinate chiefs, now threw themselves on the mercy of the government, and Tyrone, thus left destitute of adherents or resources, was at length compelled to follow their example. His first overtures were rejected by the queen, on any terms but absolute submission to her mercy in all things except his life, and even this she was prevailed on with difficulty to grant, on account of his multiplied acts of rebellion, insolence, and duplicity. But as Elizabeth's end approached, she became more susceptible of feelings of tenderness, and fresh orders were sent to the Irish viceroy to assure the earl of life, liberty, and pardon, by the title of baron Dungannon. These contradictory instructions threw lord Mountjoy for some days into a state of uncertainty, till private assurance of the queen's death pointed out to his intelligent mind, the necessity of an immediate accommodation with the great insurgent chieftain, before the diffusion of the momentous intelligence should excite a new ferment in the country. He accordingly despatched Sir William Godolphin and Sir Garret Moore to press the earl immediately to attend the viceroy, and to prevent his utter ruin by accepting the honourable conditions which he was now authorised to grant. Tyrone instantly complied with the invitation, and attending lord Mountjoy at Mellifont, he there on his knees, presented an humble and comprehensive submission in writing to the lord deputy in council, renouncing for ever the title of The O'Neil; and the viceroy on the part of the queen promised him a full pardon and the restoration of his lands, with the exception of some portions reserved for other chieftains of his family, and the use of the royal garrisons. After the conclusion of this important business Tyrone accompanied lord Mountjoy to Dublin, where, on hearing of the death of Elizabeth, he is said to have burst into a flood of tears. This emotion was ascribed by some to affection for a princess who had treated him with so much clemency, while it was attributed by others to passionate regret

for his precipitate submission, when a little
irther perseverance might have enabled him
o make his own terms with the new sovereign,
or renew the war with considerable advantage.

Thus was terminated a terrible rebellion, which for more than twenty years had spread misery, desolation and death throughout every quarter of this fair island. With its suppression fell the last vestige of the authority of the Irish princes, and its result rivetted the dominion of the English government over the country, with a firmness which no subsequent effort at insurrection has been able to shake. In its sanguinary progress the sacred name of religion was, for the first time in Ireland, made the war-whoop of party, and it has unhappily continued to be so even to our own days. But it was in the cause of the religion of the queen or the pope that the opposing factions contended; for the religion of Christ brings forth no such bitter fruits as have been recorded in the preceding pages. Indeed I am unwilling to give either party credit for pure motives in the contest. The government, for its own security, was anxious to compel the Irish by force of arms and penal laws to a conformity of worship with the sister-island, without affording them adequate means of instruction in the purer system of faith; while the Irish lords seized the moment of general insurrection thus occasioned to acquire, if possible, the sovereignty of the country: for who that reviews the proceedings of Hugh earl of Tyrone, but must agree with the assertion of Essex, at the famous conference of Dundalk, that " he cared as little for religion as his horse;" or refuse his assent to Desmond's own acknowledgment, in a repentant moment, that " he was but little instructed in religion or civility;"—and this, it is to be feared, is the character of many of the politico-religious enthusiasts of our own times. The wretched people, however, became the victims of these factions: nor had they many intervals of tranquillity under the next dynasty of English sovereigns, as you will perceive by the History of the Government of the House of Stuart in Ireland, which will afford ample materials for another Series of Stories.

END OF SECOND SERIES.

CPSIA information can be obtained
at www.ICGtesting.com
Printed in the USA
LVHW081420091219
639921LV00007B/150/P